Stories of Wonderful Hymns

By The Same Author

Stories of Favorite Hymns
Stories of Beautiful Hymns
Stories of Popular Hymns

Stories of
WONDERFUL HYMNS

Kathleen Blanchard

ZONDERVAN PUBLISHING HOUSE
GRAND RAPIDS, MICHIGAN

EIGHT FORTY-SEVEN OTTAWA AVENUE
GRAND RAPIDS, MICHIGAN

FOREWORD

This book is dedicated to the memory of those inspired men and women who gave to the world these wonderful songs. Their voices are now hushed, but their songs continue to scatter rays of sunshine and happiness across the world—a bright light to those in dark places, hope to the discouraged, and a calm harbor in the storms of life.

KATHLEEN BLANCHARD

Winnipeg, Canada

CONTENTS

Alas! And Did My Saviour Bleed 9

Almost Persuaded 11

America 12

Am I a Soldier of the Cross? 14

Anywhere with Jesus 16

Awake, My Soul, Stretch Every Nerve 17

Blessed Assurance 19

Break Thou the Bread of Life 20

Carol, Sweetly Carol 22

Christ Returneth 23

Come, Thou Almighty King 25

Count Your Blessings 26

Dare to Be a Daniel 28

Depth of Mercy! Can There Be 29

From Heaven Above to Earth I Come 31

He Leadeth Me 33

Hiding in Thee 35

I Gave My Life for Thee 36

I Know That My Redeemer Lives 38

I'm Praying for You 40

I Must Tell Jesus 41

In the Land of Strangers 43

I've Found a Friend 45

Jesus Is Tenderly Calling 46

Jesus, Keep Me Near the Cross 48

Jesus Loves Me 49

Jesus of Nazareth Passeth By 51

Jesus Saves! Jesus Saves! 53

Jesus, Still Lead On 54

Jesus, These Eyes Have Never Seen 56

Contents

Joy to the World 57
Let the Lower Lights Be Burning 59
Like Silver Lamps in a Distant Shrine 60
Master, the Tempest Is Raging 62
More Holiness Give Me 64
Nothing But Leaves 65
Oh, for a Faith 67
O Master, Let Me Walk with Thee 68
On Christ, the Solid Rock, I Stand 69
One More Day's Work for Jesus 71
Pass It On 73
Pass Me Not 75
Rescue the Perishing 76
Ring the Bells of Heaven 78
Saviour, Like a Shepherd Lead Us 79
Saviour, Sprinkle Many Nations 81
Soldiers of Christ, Arise 83
Sweet Hour of Prayer 84
Take Me As I Am 86
Tell Me the Old, Old Story 88
Tell Mother I'll Be There 90
The Light of the World Is Jesus 92
The Morning Bright 93
The Ninety and Nine 95
The Son of God Goes Forth to War 97
Thou Art Gone to the Grave 99
'Tis So Sweet to Trust In Jesus 100
True-Hearted, Whole-Hearted 101
We Would See Jesus 103
What a Wonderful Saviour! 104
When the Roll Is Called Up Yonder 106
Why Do You Wait? 107

ALAS! AND DID MY SAVIOUR BLEED*

ISAAC WATTS was a thin, spare man about five feet, three inches tall. He had a low forehead, prominent cheek bones and small gray eyes. When in repose his face had a rather heavy look. His biographers record that his voice was clear and excellent, his speech polished and graceful.

Watts was born at Southampton, England, the eldest of a family of nine children. He was a delicate child, did not take readily to games, but was a lover of books and poetry.

In July, 1698, at the age of twenty-four, he preached his first sermon at Mark Lane Independent Church. While serving there as pastor his health gave way—partly, it was said, because the lady whom he was about to marry changed her mind. He was engaged to Miss Elizabeth Sayer, but at the last moment she decided in favor of an older man, a schoolmaster named Thomas Rowe.

During the next few years Watts was frequently ill. However, kind friends came to his aid. Sir Thomas and Lady Abney invited him to be their guest at their lovely country home within reach of London, and there it was that Watts wrote many of his famous hymns, including the one given here.

When Watts was thirty years old, another loved hymn-writer was born, whose name was Doddridge. In later life the two became friends and each enriched his generation with outstanding hymns.

* Copyright 1926. Renewal. Mrs. Mary Hudson.

Fanny Crosby related that the singing of this hymn induced her to make her choice for Christ. It was at a Gospel meeting in a Methodist church which she had attended with friends.

"I arose and went forward alone," she said. "After prayer the congregation began to sing the grand old consecration hymn of Isaac Watts. I surrendered myself to the Saviour, and my very soul was flooded with celestial light. I sprang to my feet and shouted 'Hallelujah!' as the last lines of the hymn spoke for me: 'Here, Lord, I give myself away—'tis all that I can do.'"

> Alas! and did my Saviour bleed,
>   And did my Sovereign die,
> Would He devote that sacred head
>   For such a worm as I?
>
> Was it for crimes that I had done
>   He groaned upon the tree?
> Amazing pity! grace unknown!
>   And love beyond degree!
>
> Well might the sun in darkness hide,
>   And shut his glories in,
> When Christ, the great Creator, died
>   For man, the creature's sin.
>
> Thus might I hide my blushing face
>   While His dear Cross appears;
> Dissolve my heart in thankfulness,
>   And melt my eyes to tears.
>
> But drops of grief can ne'er repay
>   The debt of love I owe;
> Here, Lord, I give myself away—
>   'Tis all that I can do.

* * *

ALMOST PERSUADED

PHILIP PAUL BLISS was one of a group of sweet singers whose songs have been sung in every corner of the earth. These singers came on a wave of spiritual awakening in the middle of the nineteenth century. They believed in the power of spiritual song.

Philip Bliss was a descendent of Puritans. He learned to play melodies on reeds cut from the marshes. So fond was he of sweet sounds that once when he was a barefoot boy selling vegetables at a house, he left his basket at the sound of music and climbed the garden fence to stand spellbound by an open window. There he listened until the startled player sent him away.

In his youth Bliss attended a musical convention in Rome, Pennsylvania. Here he met William H. Bradbury, a pioneer in American Gospel hymnody, and a well-known musician. Philip Bliss made up his mind to spend his life in Gospel service.

The time came when he was using his talent in conjunction with Dwight L. Moody. One Sunday evening he walked down the street of a little town where he had just arrived until he came to a lighted church. A service was in progress and he slipped into the back seat. His attention was soon arrested by a dramatic reading of the twenty-sixth chapter of the Acts of the Apostles, and especially by these words of Paul to King Agrippa:

"For the king knoweth of these things, before whom also I speak freely: for I am persuaded that none of these things are hidden from him; for this thing was not done in a corner. King Agrippa, believest thou the prophets? I know that thou believest. Then Agrippa said to Paul, Almost thou persuadest me to be a Christian. And Paul said, I would to God, that not only thou, but also all that hear me this day, were both almost, and altogether such as I am, except these bonds."

Philip Bliss said that the verses of this hymn began to form in his mind even before he left the church.

It is a far cry from that age to this. But the visitors to Cyprus see there the church, hewn out of the solid rock, where early Christians worshiped in secret; and the marble pillar (now surrounded by an iron railing) to which Paul was bound and beaten when he landed on the island.

"Almost persuaded," now to believe;
"Almost persuaded," Christ to receive;
  Seems now some soul to say:
"Go, Spirit, go Thy way,
  Some more convenient day
    On Thee I'll call."

"Almost persuaded," come, come today;
"Almost persuaded," turn not away;
  Jesus invites you here,
  Angels are lingering near,
  Prayers rise from hearts so dear,
    O wanderer, come.

"Almost persuaded," harvest is past!
"Almost persuaded," doom comes at last!
"Almost" cannot avail;
"Almost" is but to fail!
  Sad, sad, that bitter wail,
    "Almost," but lost.

*   *   *

AMERICA

SAMUEL FRANCIS SMITH was born in Boston, in 1808. He was graduated from Harvard at the age of twenty-one, then went to Andover Theological Seminary to study for the Baptist ministry.

Samuel was a linguist, and also a poet. He had a con-
genial intimate in the musical Lowell Mason. Many pleasant hours the friends spent together in music and song—
trying various compositions gathered from many sources.

In the early part of 1832—so the story goes—his friend
Mason brought Smith a book of German songs to translate.
The air written by Henry Carey for George II, and known
in England as "God Save the King" intrigued him. "I
thought," he related, "why cannot we have a patriotic
hymn?"

He seized a pencil and paper and "in half an hour it was
written"—the four stanzas now known the world over as
"America."

Who was Carey? He was a popular musician of the day
who pleased music-loving people by writing a song that was
on everyone's lips, "Sally in Our Alley."

Henry Carey died, however, before he secured recognition as the anonymous writer of the patriotic anthem "God
Save the King." But later on his son laid claim before the
new King, George III, who granted him a sum of money
from his privy purse.

*   *   *

In 1887, Dr. Smith, happened to be in Chicago, and was
being shown over the great wheat pit. While he followed
the business from the gallery as an interested spectator,
suddenly the trading ceased and the author heard his familiar words, "My country, 'tis of thee." Midst cheers and ac-
clamation from the floor, the men stood with hats off as they
sang the hymn through.

The song was arranged for use by Lowell Mason, who
entitled it "America." It was published in the *Psalmist* in
1843, nine years after it was written.

> My country! 'tis of thee,
> Sweet land of liberty,
>   Of thee I sing;

Land where my fathers died!
Land of the Pilgrims' pride!
From every mountain side
    Let freedom ring!

My native country, thee—
Land of the noble, free—
    Thy name I love;
I love thy rocks and rills,
Thy woods and templed hills;
My heart with rapture thrills
    Like that above.

Let music swell the breeze,
And ring from all the trees
    Sweet freedom's song:
Let mortal tongues awake;
Let all that breathe partake;
Let rocks their silence break,
    The sound prolong.

Our fathers' God, to Thee,
Author of liberty,
    To Thee we sing:
Long may our land be bright
With freedom's holy light;
Protect us by Thy might,
    Great God, our King!

*   *   *

AM I A SOLDIER OF THE CROSS?

BORN IN 1674, in the stormy days of Nonconformity, Isaac
Watts was the founder of modern church singing. Although
his hymns were numerous only a few have gained print.

In spite of ill health during most of his seventy-five years,
Watts lived in happy circumstances at the home of his fast
friends, Sir Thomas and Lady Abney. And there it was that
he wrote many of his hymns.

In his early years when studying for the Nonconformist

church, Watts became tutor to the children of Sir John Hartopp, and throughout the years, they always showed a warm friendship for their former kindly and tolerant master.

The young man, Doddridge, who was also a Nonconformist minister, and afflicted, too, with poor health, formed a profound admiration for Isaac Watts who was his senior by thirty years, but with whom he had much in common.

Whenever Doddridge heard a new hymn by Isaac Watts, he would write to congratulate him. Here is an extract from one such letter: "On Tuesday last I was preaching to a large assembly of plain country people at a village a few miles off, when after a sermon from Hebrews 6, we sang one of your hymns. I had the satisfaction to observe tears in the eyes of several of the people."

Isaac Watts wrote this hymn in 1709. That Sunday morning his congregation at Mark Lane Church had been arrested by his earnest sermon on the Christian warfare as portrayed in the lesson for that day, I Corinthians 16:13, "Watch ye, stand fast in the faith, quit you like men, be strong."

No one knew better than Watts the power of song upon the masses, but it was many years before joyful melody became the custom in churches.

The hymns of Watts are as popular today as when they were written two hundred years ago.

> Am I a soldier of the Cross,
>   A follower of the Lamb?
> And shall I fear to own His cause,
>   Or blush to speak His Name?
>
> Must I be carried to the skies
>   On flowery beds of ease?
> While others fought to win the prize,
>   And sailed through bloody seas?

Are there no foes for me to face?
  Must I not stem the flood?
Is this vile world a friend to grace,
  To help me on to God?

Sure I must fight, if I would reign;
  Increase my courage, Lord!
I'll bear the toil, endure the pain,
  Supported by Thy Word.

Thy saints, in all this glorious war,
  Shall conquer, though they die;
They view the triumph from afar,
  And seize it with their eye.

When that illustrious day shall rise,
  And all Thine armies shine
In robes of victory through the skies,
  The glory shall be Thine.

* * *

ANYWHERE WITH JESUS

THE AUTHOR of this hymn was Mrs. Jessie Pounds, born
in Hiram, near Cleveland, in 1861. When only fifteen she
began to write in local periodicals sacred lyrics suitable
for hymns, especially for use in evangelistic meetings.

The editor of a hymnal, J. H. Filmore, invited Jessie
Pounds to write some hymns suitable for a book he hoped
to bring out soon—an invitation which prompted her to
devote herself seriously to hymn composition.

Soon people everywhere were singing her songs with
their tuneful airs—hymns such as "The Way of the Cross
Leads Home," and "Beautiful Isle of Somewhere." The
latter was in great request and was sung at many funeral
services, including that of President McKinley.

Jessie Pounds often related the little story of the way the
words of this hymn came to her mind. "It was one Sunday
morning in 1897," she said; "not feeling well enough to go

to church I sat in my room, musing, and before I was
scarcely aware of it, I wrote down these lines as they stand
today."

The words were set to music by that skillful composer,
D. B. Towner, who is also remembered for the tune to
"Trust and Obey."

Anywhere with Jesus I can safely go;
Anywhere He leads me in this world below;
Anywhere without Him dearest joys would fade;
Anywhere with Jesus I am not afraid.

(Chorus)
Anywhere! anywhere! Fear I cannot know;
Anywhere with Jesus I can safely go.

Anywhere with Jesus I am not alone;
Other friends may fail me, He is still my own;
Tho' His hand may lead me over dreary ways,
Anywhere with Jesus is a house of praise.

Anywhere with Jesus over land and sea,
Telling souls in darkness of salvation free;
Ready as He summons me to go or stay,
Anywhere with Jesus when He points the way.

Anywhere with Jesus I can go to sleep,
When the dark'ning shadows round about me creep;
Knowing I shall waken, never more to roam,
Anywhere with Jesus will be home, sweet home.

* Copyright 1915. Renewal. Hope Publishing Company, owner.

*   *   *

AWAKE, MY SOUL, STRETCH EVERY NERVE

LONG AGO the Greeks chose the springtime of the year for
the Olympic games, contests of which the youth of cities
such as Athens and Sparta dreamed from childhood. What
glory and honor would be theirs if they won the race!

The victor would be crowned with an olive wreath and
was so renowned that he was held too great to enter the
city by the gate. A special entrance must be made in the

wall where none but he might pass! A special seat at festivals and all gala functions was provided for him and—by no means least in the honors accorded—his statue adorned the sacred grove of Olympia.

As the day of the games drew near men of every rank from all over Greece gathered there. Poets and princes with their caravans wended their way to behold the spectacle and to applaud the winner.

On a Sunday morning in the year 1705, Philip Doddridge had read the lesson from I Corinthians where Paul used the Greek athletic games to illustrate the Christian's course on earth.

The young minister of Kibworth was a most earnest teacher and preacher. Most of his congregation could neither read nor write, but he had overcome that difficulty by having the people repeat the words of the hymn after him, until they were firmly impressed on their minds.

Many of the manuscripts of Doddridge are still extant—beautifully written in a clear firm hand—and with the ink upon them quite unfaded.

> Awake, my soul, stretch every nerve
>   And press with vigor on;
> A heavenly race demands thy zeal,
>   And an immortal crown.
>
> A cloud of witnesses around
>   Hold thee in full survey;
> Forget the steps already trod,
>   And onward urge thy way.
>
> 'Tis God's all-animating voice,
>   That calls thee from on high,
> 'Tis His own hand presents the prize
>   To thine aspiring eye.
>
> Blest Saviour, introduced by Thee,
>   Have I my race begun;
> And, crown'd with victory, at Thy feet
>   I'll lay my honors down.

*   *   *

BLESSED ASSURANCE

MANY PEOPLE are quite unaware of the treasures to be found in their hymnbooks. That is a pity, as we seldom forget the hymns of our youth. They wind invisible threads about us and are the language of the heart.

Fanny Crosby was thankful for the great gift of heavenly love which endowed her life in such a powerful way in the Master's service. There was something about Fanny Crosby's hymns that stayed in people's minds. There is a story that when this hymn was once sung at the Convention Hall, Minneapolis, the various delegations that had traveled to the meeting sang it on their way out, and as far as the railway station—even on the train as they left.

Sankey had a great regard for the blind poetess, and made the statement that "there were few who brought me more joy and peace in my heart than Fanny Crosby." The poetess met Ira D. Sankey in the early days of the evangelist's career, and he set to music many of her hymns and used them in his meetings.

In later life Sankey, too, became blind, and often recalled the wonderful character and faith of his old friend, Fanny Crosby.

The haunting tune set to Fanny Crosby's words was composed by Mrs. J. F. Knapp.

> Blessed assurance, Jesus is mine!
> Oh, what a foretaste of glory divine!
> Heir of salvation, purchase of God,
> Born of His Spirit, washed in His blood.
>
> (Chorus)
> This is my story, this is my song;
> Praising my Saviour all the day long;
> This is my story, this is my song,
> Praising my Saviour all the day long.

Perfect submission, perfect delight,
Visions of rapture now burst on my sight,
Angels descending, bring from above
Echoes of mercy, whispers of love.

Perfect submission, all is at rest,
I in my Saviour am happy and blest,
Watching and waiting, looking above,
Filled with His goodness, lost in His love.

*   *   *

BREAK THOU THE BREAD OF LIFE

MARY ARTEMISIA LATHBURY was born in 1841. She spent her early life in Manchester, New York.

Her father was a preacher of the Methodist Episcopal church. Her two brothers were ministers in the same denomination.

Mary Lathbury was a skilled artist, who expressed her thoughts in verse for various children's periodicals, for she loved young people.

Another interest in her life was the "Look Up Legion," which she founded in Sunday schools of her church. The little ones were taught to look "up" and not "down," to look "out" and not "in."

The Chautauqua movement was very near to her heart, and she looked forward to these gatherings with great happiness. She was welcomed there as "Laureate of Chautauqua."

One day in the summer of 1880, Mary had been reading again the beautiful story, in Matthew 15:29-39, of Christ by the sea of Galilee. He had been followed by a vast and curious concourse of people, many of whom had terrible troubles that they hoped he would heal. Though the day was far spent and they had had nothing to eat for three days, they refused to leave. Jesus knew their wants and filled with compassion, satisfied them.

In the beautiful surroundings of Bishop Vincent's College on the lake shore, Mary Lathbury could well imagine the scene of the miracle by the Sea of Galilee.

The hymn was written, and passed round the "Literary and Scientific Club" of that college. It became well known and is loved on both sides of the Atlantic and may be found in most collections.

Break Thou the bread of life,
    Dear Lord to me,
As Thou didst break the loaves
    Beside the sea;
Beyond the sacred page
    I seek Thee, Lord;
My spirit pants for Thee,
    O living Word!

Bless Thou the truth, dear Lord,
    To me—to me—
As Thou didst bless the bread
    By Galilee;
Then shall all bondage cease,
    All fetters fall;
And I shall find my peace,
    My All-in-All!

Thou art the bread of life,
    O Lord, to me,
Thy holy Word the truth
    That saveth me;
Give me to eat and live,
    With Thee above;
Teach me to love Thy truth,
    For Thou art love.

O, send Thy Spirit, Lord,
    Now unto me,
That He may touch my eyes,
    And make me see:
Show me the truth concealed
    Within Thy Word,
And in Thy Book revealed
    I see the Lord.

*   *   *

CAROL, SWEETLY CAROL

No OTHER writing is quite like a hymn. It is the expression of feeling within—sometimes the philosophy of a lifetime summed up in a few words.

So it was with Fanny Crosby, the blind poetess. She maintained that hymns fasten upon the imagination and ease the mind. A familiar tune may arrest the attention and perhaps start a tear, as memory gently draws back the curtain from scenes of long ago.

It was when Fanny Crosby was about forty-five-years of age that she gave up song writing and determined in the future to write only hymns. In this she found her true vocation, for she related that she was happy every day of her life. From her blindness she seemed to derive deep insight into reality. Who can estimate the good her words have accomplished?

It was just a year after writing "Safe in the Arms of Jesus"—perhaps the favorite of her hymns—when one day toward the Chistmas season Fanny Crosby attended a Bible meeting. The leader read Psalm 100 in a voice full of meaning: "Make a joyful noise unto the Lord, all ye lands . . . come before his presence with singing."

It seemed that she was lifted into an ecstasy of praise to the Maker of all things. In this entranced mood she expressed the angelic story poetically. Quickly her friends took down the words that fell from her lips almost faster than they could be written.

This is the carol.

Carol, sweetly carol,
  A Saviour born today;
Bear the joyful tidings,
  O bear them far away:
Carol, sweetly carol,
  Till earth's remotest bound
Shall hear the mighty chorus,
  And echo back the sound.

(Chorus)
Carol, sweetly carol,
   Carol sweetly today,
Bear the joyful tidings,
   O bear them far away.

Carol, sweetly carol,
   As when the angel throng
O'er the vales of Judah
   Awoke the heavenly song:
Carol, sweetly carol,
   Good will and peace and love,
Glory in the highest,
   To God who reigns above.

Carol, sweetly carol,
   The happy Christmas time;
Hark! the bells are pealing
   Their merry, merry chime:
Carol, sweetly carol,
   Ye shining ones above,
Sing in loudest numbers
   O sing redeeming love.

*   *   *

CHRIST RETURNETH

MANY PEOPLE who love hymns, find that they prove a
solace when the heart is aching. They leave a peace in the
rush of everyday life, and cast a halo over common things.

James McGranahan, a colleague of Sankey and one of
his band of evangelists, wrote many hymns, also suitable
melodies for them, which were sung everywhere. McGranahan was one of the foremost composers of evangelistic
songs of his time and Sankey made the hymns famous.

When Moody and Sankey traveled across the water they
went armed with bundles of sacred songs . . . America was
the home of the new singing.

One of the most popular of McGranahan's songs, was

"Sometime We'll Understand." Time and again when this was sung, Sankey related, there was a request to have it again.

On Moody's and Sankey's second mission to England in 1883, both Stebbins and McGranahan joined the circle abroad—a circle which at home in Chicago included Moody, Sankey, Bliss, Whittle, McGranahan, Case, Excell, Gabriel and Stebbins. These were men whose evangelistic fervor inspired the masses. They trained the youth to love singing —and thousands answered the call.

The following hymn was written by H. L. Turner. McGranahan liked the words so much that he set it to the tune we know.

> It may be at morn, when the day is awaking,
> When sunlight thro' darkness and shadow is breaking,
>   That Jesus will come in the fullness of glory,
> To receive from the world His own.
>
>   (Chorus)
>   O Lord Jesus, how long,
>   How long ere we shout the glad song?
>   Christ returneth,
>   Christ returneth, hallelujah! Amen,
>   Hallelujah! Amen.
>
> It may be at midday, it may be at twilight,
> It may be, perchance, that the blackness of midnight
> Will burst into light in the blaze of His glory,
> When Jesus receives His own.
>
> While hosts cry Hosanna, from heaven descending,
> With glorified saints and the angels attending,
> With grace on His brow, like a halo of glory,
> Will Jesus receive His own.
>
> Oh, joy! oh, delight! should we go without dying,
> No sickness, no sadness, no dread, and no crying,
> Caught up through the clouds with our Lord into glory,
> When Jesus receives His own.

*   *   *

COME, THOU ALMIGHTY KING

CHARLES WESLEY'S MOTHER was Susannah Annesley the twenty-fifth child of the Nonconformist minister, Dr. Samuel Annesly, who was chaplain at the Nonconformist Chapel at Bishopsgate, London, England.

Susannah, a determined young woman, meant to marry the Anglican curate she had met—Samuel Wesley. At the marriage of the famous pair Susannah became Anglican.

In due course the Rev. Samuel Wesley was given the rectory of Epworth, with Wrote, Lincolnshire. The rector was not very successful in farming his glebe, and instead of making money, went steadily into debt.

John was the fifteenth child of the family and Charles was the youngest living member of the eighteen children. The eldest boy, Samuel, was a tower of strength to the younger boys. However, the world did not hear much of Samuel.

There were seven sisters at the rectory, and it had been impressed upon them that John and Charles were meant for something great. The sisters must cheerfully make every sacrifice for these two brothers. Strict food rationing was necessary because of their poverty.

After years of "going without," the mother died. Charles' favorite sister, Hetty, related that they sang a hymn as they had promised and that the faces of John and Charles were radiant and transfigured with joy of their faith.

Then suddenly she saw the purpose of their common suffering. The years of pinching and starving, the thousand vexations that had worn the dear mother down, her own sorrowful fate and that of her sisters—the purpose was John, whose hand clasped the sword which was to pierce the heart of England.

The following hymn was found printed on a little leaflet in 1775, in company with two Wesley hymns, Martin Madan

published it in 1763. Lady Huntingdon's cousin, Walter
Shirley, used it. These were all Charles Wesley's friends.
The hymn, though unsigned, is ascribed to Charles Wesley,
but was not in their *Collection.*

Come, Thou Almighty King,
Help us Thy Name to sing,
  Help us to praise:
Father! all-glorious,
O'er all victorious,
Come, and reign over us,
  Ancient of Days!

Come, Thou incarnate Word,
Gird on Thy mighty sword;
  Our prayer attend;
Come, and Thy people bless,
And give Thy Word success;
Spirit of holiness,
  On us descend.

Come, holy Comforter!
Thy sacred witness bear,
  In this glad hour:
Thou, who almighty art,
Now rule in every heart,
And ne'er from us depart,
  Spirit of power!

To the great One in Three,
The highest praises be,
  Hence evermore!
His sovereign majesty
May we in glory see,
And to eternity
  Love and adore.

*   *   *

COUNT YOUR BLESSINGS

MOODY AND SANKEY—those great evangelists of a few
decades ago—made good use of the tunes of the negro race.
These tunes express deep emotions, and never failed to

reach the hearts of the evangelists' audiences—both on this side of the water, and overseas.

E. O. Excell, who was born in Stark County, Ohio, in 1857 was one of the devoted band of workers whom Moody and Sankey could always draw upon.

Excell had to work hard as a lad, for a bricklayer master saw to it that he was kept busy. Nevertheless, nothing could prevent the lad from singing. Having reached man's estate, Excell broke away from manual work, and began to study, making the Sunday school his chief concern. He wrote many hymns—both words and music—for the children.

Then the day came when he widened his life and became a singing evangelist. He never failed to secure a sympathetic hearing, for his songs were like angels' voices. People flocked to hear his beautiful appealing voice . . . and when he had moved his hearers' emotions, he showed them the way to another world.

Mr. Moody persuaded him to join his mission. Excell did so and composed many tunes which were used at the Moody and Sankey services. This hymn—the words of which were written by a Wesleyan minister, Johnson Oatman—was one of them.

The time came when Excell lay sick in a hospital in Chicago. His old friend Charles Gabriel, who wrote the Glory Song, visited him and the two friends lived their songs over again and sang together for the last time the melodies they loved.

> When upon life's billows you are tempest-tossed,
> When you are discouraged, thinking all is lost,
> Count your many blessings, name them one by one,
> And it will surprise you what the Lord hath done.
>
> (Chorus)
> Count your blessings, name them one by one;
> Count your blessings, see what God has done!
> Count your blessings, name them one by one;
> Count your many blessings, see what God hath done

Are you ever burdened with a load of care?
Does the cross seem heavy you are called to bear?
Count your many blessings, every doubt will fly,
And you will keep singing as the days go by.

When you look at others with their lands and gold,
Think that Christ has promised you His wealth untold.
Count your many blessings, every doubt will fly,
Your reward in heaven, nor your home on high.

So, amid the conflict, whether great or small,
Do not be disheartened, God is over all;
Count your many blessings, angels will attend,
Help and comfort give you to your journey's end.

* Copyright 1925. Renewal. Hope Publishing Company, owner.

* * *

DARE TO BE A DANIEL

PHILIP PAUL BLISS wrote many hymns, both words and music, all of which have a strange haunting appeal.

There are always people to whom a certain hymn brings memories, for there is a subtle influence in words which are sung.

Bliss taught that love and courage will help us walk the daily round of life, and that the power of spiritual songs will pave the way to knowledge of another world, through the emotions.

One writer has expressed the opinion that though some of the hymns may be doggerel poetry, faulty in grammar and wrong in theology, yet, if any particular hymn has proved itself a staff and stay to some heroic soul in the dark hours of life, then that hymn has won its right to a place among the sacred songs through which God speaks to the souls of men.

Among the famous Victorians who testified to the power of hymns was Edna Lyall, one of the novelists of that era.

After she had heard the following hymn sung, she secured a copy and read it through.

"I can certainly say," she testified "that the refrain 'Dare to Be a Daniel' has helped me again and again. I do not know the rest of the hymn well, and some of it you may not like, still I like it for the good it has done."

Bliss wrote this hymn for his Sunday school class in the First Congregational Church of Chicago. The hymn was often used at the Moody and Sankey meetings, always with good effect.

Standing by a purpose true,
    Heeding God's command,
Honor them, the faithful few!
    All hail to Daniel's band!

(Chorus)
Dare to be a Daniel!
    Dare to stand alone!
Dare to have a purpose firm!
    Dare to make it known!

Many mighty men are lost,
    Daring not to stand,
Who for God had been a host,
    By joining Daniel's band.

Many giants, great and tall,
    Stalking through the land,
Headlong to the earth would fall,
    If met by Daniel's band.

Hold the Gospel banner high!
    On to victory grand!
Satan and his host defy,
    And shout for Daniel's band!

* * *

DEPTH OF MERCY! CAN THERE BE

THE HIGHEST FORM of love endeavors only to bestow, and loses itself in so doing.

This practical Chirstianity was what the Wesleys insisted upon. John preached it, and Charles wrote of it, "For," said he, "the beautiful exists in the most abandoned sinner and each human soul possesses creative power which he can use for good or ill."

Charles Wesley called his hymns poetical Scripture. They brought comfort and consolation to many of the sad and weary on earth. He was so versed in hymn writing that he unconciously turned any subject of the moment into the language of sacred song.

The story is told that one evening—after one of their meetings— their way home led over the cobblestoned streets of a little town and past a public house. Noisy voices, loud laughter and singing arrested their steps. Musical Charles was fascinated by the tune and said to his friends, "Why should the devil have a tune like that all to himself?"

He immediately picked up the air and composed at the same time words to suit the melody. When it was completed he remarked gleefully that he had taken something from the devil for the Lord's work.

This hymn, which may be found in the *Moody and Sankey Hymn Book*, was the result of that experience.

> Depth of mercy! can there be
> Mercy still reserved for me?
> Can my God His wrath forbear?
> Me, the chief of sinners, spare?
>
> I have long withstood His grace;
> Long provoked Him to His face:
> Would not hearken to His calls;
> Grieved Him by a thousand falls.
>
> Whence to me this waste of love?
> Ask my Advocate above!
> See the cause in Jesus' face,
> Now before the throne of grace.
>
> There for me the Saviour stands;
> Shows His wounds, and spreads His hands;

God is love, I know, I feel;
Jesus pleads, and loves me still.

If I rightly read Thy heart,
If Thou all compassion art,
Bow Thine ear, in mercy bow,
Pardon and accept me now.

*　　*　　*

FROM HEAVEN ABOVE TO EARTH I COME

AT EISENACH, GERMANY, before World War II began, there was still to be seen the schoolroom where Martin Luther attended. Luther was fond of fun—like many other boys of his age—and enjoyed jokes. It was said that his sweet voice always gained him friends and got out of scrapes

It was quite a walk into Eisenach to school, as the Luther family lived outside near the mine where the father worked. The schoolmaster, Trebonius, had a habit of lifting his hat to his scholars each morning, because, as he put it, the great ones of the future were among them.

After a lapse of years, Luther lived at Wittenberg—where he was a professor. His chair, table and stove have been jealously guarded.

Martin Luther possessed a strong physique and a powerful personality. He had broad shoulders, a thick neck and large piercing eyes, and above all, a kindly countenance and very fresh complexion. He was habitually garbed in a monk's dress rather the worse for wear.

His strength of character made him stand out distinctly among the great personalities of the day. It was the age of the scholar Erasmus, who had written much and set the world talking; and in England, Master Thomas More cried out against the evils of the age. But is was the Augustinian monk who challenged the forces of evil to mortal combat!

In Wittenberg, on the spot where Luther burned the papal

bull, there is a great oak tree growing. A living symbol of Luther, it spreads out its branches on all sides. It was planted many years ago to commemorate the deed. The Castle Church of Wittenberg—on whose door he nailed the Proclamation of Reformation—is the place where his remains rest.

Luther had five children. His devoted wife helped the family budget by working in the garden and keeping boarders.

Luther wrote this Christmas carol expressly for his little son Hans. He arranged for a man dressed as an angel to sing the first three verses. On Christmas Eve the family was surprised by this earthly angel . . . Luther took up the refrain and helped with the singing.

This carol was published in Wittenberg, in 1535. So popular did it become that four years later Luther wrote suitable music for it.

Miss Winkworth translated it for her Lyra Germanica. It bore the heading "The Father Sent the Son to Be the Saviour of the World."

> From heaven above to earth I come,
> To bear good news to every home;
> Glad tidings of great joy I bring,
> Whereof I now will say and sing—

> "To you this night is born a child
> Of Mary, chosen Mother mild;
> This little child of lowly birth,
> Shall be the joy of all your earth.

> " 'Tis Christ our God, who far on high
> Hath heard your sad and bitter cry;
> Himself will your Salvation be;
> Himself from sin will make you free.

> "He brings those blessings, long ago
> Prepared by God for all below:
> Henceforth His kingdom open stands
> To you, as to the angel bands.

"Welcome to earth, Thou noble Guest,
Through whom even wicked men are blest
Thou com'st to share our misery;
What can we render, Lord, to Thee?

"Were earth a thousand times as fair,
Beset with gold and jewels rare,
She yet were far too poor to be
A narrow cradle, Lord, for Thee.

"Ah! dearest Jesus, Holy Child,
Make Thee a bed, soft undefiled,
Within my heart that it may be
A quiet chamber kept for Thee.

"My heart for very joy doth leap;
My lips no more can silence keep;
I too must raise with joyful tongue
That sweetest ancient cradle song.

" 'Glory to God in highest heaven,
Who unto man His Son hath given!'
While angels sing with pious mirth
A glad New Year to all the earth."

* * *

HE LEADETH ME

THIS WONDERFUL HYMN and the accompanying tune was the work of two remarkable men who labored greatly in the Master's service.

The words were written by Joseph H. Gilmore, who has related how the hymn was given to the world.

"It was the year 1862. I was talking at the Wednesday evening lecture of the First Baptist Church of Philadelphia," he wrote.

"The talk was on the Twenty-Third Psalm, and I had been especially impressed with the blessedness of being led by God, of the mere fact of His leadership, altogether apart from the way in which He leads us and what He is leading

us to. At the close of the service we adjourned to Deacon
Watsons's home, where I was staying.

"The blessedness of God's leadership so grew upon me
that I took out my pencil, wrote the hymn just as it stands
today, handed it to my wife and thought no more about it.
She sent it to *The Watchman and Reflector*, who published
it.

"Three years later I went to Rochester to preach for the
Second Baptist Church. On entering the chapel I took up
a hymnbook, for I thought, 'I wonder what they sing.' The
book opened at 'He Leadeth Me,' and that was the first time
I knew my hymn had found a place among the songs of the
church. I shall never forget the impression made upon me
by coming then and there in contact with my own assertion
of God's leadership."

The composer of the melody to which these words were
set was W. B. Bradbury. When Bradbury was young and
poor it was Lowell Mason who helped him greatly in the
musical world, and in befriending Bradbury he helped the
whole world of sacred song, for it is due to the music-loving
Bradbury that we have so many arresting and lasting tunes.

One day while idly turning over the leaves of a journal he
had seen this hymn and had cut it out. In due course it was
set to the melody that the world knows.

> He leadeth me: O blessed thought!
> O words with heavenly comfort fraught!
> Whate'er I do, where'er I be,
> Still 'tis God's hand that leadeth me.
>
> (Chorus)
> He leadeth me! He leadeth me!
> For by His hand He leadeth me.
> His faithful follower I would be,
> For by his hand He leadeth me.
>
> Sometimes 'mid scenes of deepest gloom,
> Sometimes where Eden's bowers bloom,
> By waters still o'er troubled sea,
> Still 'tis God's hand that leadeth me.

Lord, I would clasp Thy hand in mine,
Nor ever murmur nor repine;
Content, whatever lot I see,
Since 'tis my God that leadeth me.

And when my task on earth is done,
When by Thy grace the victory's won,
E'en death's cold wave I will not flee,
Since God through Jordon leadeth me.

*   *   *

HIDING IN THEE

IN 1876, when this hymn was written, William O. Cushing was living at a little place named Moravia, in New York State.

Cushing was a well-known evangelist, musician and composer of sacred songs. From his pen flowed melodious words and music, so arresting in their earnestness that they held the listeners' attention and profoundly influenced them. One of the favorites is "Beautiful Valley of Eden," written the year previous.

One day, Ira D. Sankey had sent him an earnest appeal for a hymn to be used at his meetings. William Cushing could not ignore such an appeal. Hymns are the language of the heart; they are the expression of hope, trust, longing, sorrow, joy and even of despair of the soul.

"I prayed about it," he said. "After a little time had elapsed, one day when at prayer, something seemed to form in my mind, and as the result of many soul-yearning conflicts within, and tears of which the world can never know, these words were put into my mind."

The hymn was soon put to music by Ira D. Sankey, who sang it into people's hearts. It is still much used, especially at evangelistic meetings.

Oh, safe to the Rock that is higher than I,
My soul in its conflicts and sorrows would fly;
So sinful, so weary, Thine, Thine would I be;
Thou blest "Rock of Ages," I'm hiding in Thee.

(Chorus)
Hiding in Thee, hiding in Thee,
Thou blest "Rock of Ages," I'm hiding in Thee.

In the calm of the noontide, in sorrow's lone hour,
In times when temptation casts o'er me its power;
In the tempests of life, on its wide, heaving sea,
Thou blest "Rock of Ages," I'm hiding in Thee.

How oft in the conflict, when pressed by the foe,
I have fled to my Refuge and breathed out my woe;
How often when trials like sea billows roll,
Have I hidden in Thee, O Thou Rock of my soul.

* * *

I GAVE MY LIFE FOR THEE

The value of the legacy which Frances Ridley Havergal, left to humanity is beyond reckoning.

The youngest child of the family of Rev. W. H. Havergal, she was petted and made much of, partly on account of delicacy of health, and because she was such a lovable child. But this did not spoil her character, as from her teens she seemed to have felt conscious of religion, and to have desired a life of service to others.

Never strong, her constitution was taxed to the utmost by her arduous and varied labors and correspondence. During one of her sick bouts, she remarked to her friends that she hoped the angels would leave her alone for a little while when she got to heaven.

Not only in poetry did Frances Havergal excel, but in music also. She set some of her poems to melody. Her religious spirit was a buoyant one, and all her hymns are manifestations of that serene happiness she had been able to achieve. Her song of faith and praise never tired; she had a living joy in serving her Master.

Once in speaking to friends of her early life, she related that when she was fourteen all her morbidness, fears and doubts seemed to be lifted, and ever afterward nothing but happiness filled her being.

Her well-known hymn "I Gave My Life for Thee" first appeared in *Good Words*. It was written in Germany when Frances was staying there with friends.

It was in the year 1888, according to her sister, that Frances had come in weary, and had sat down opposite a picture with that motto. At once the lines flashed upon her, and she wrote them in pencil on a scrap of paper. When she read them over, they did not satisfy her. She tossed them into the fire, but they fell out unmarked. Some months later she showed them to her father and he encouraged her to preserve them. He wrote the tune "Baca" especially for them.

Her life work finished, Frances Ridley Havergal died at Caswall Bay, near Swansea, England. She was only forty-three. The many hymns that she wrote will continue to live and bring comfort to all who use them.

> I gave My life for thee,
>   My precious blood I shed,
> That thou might'st ransomed be,
>   And quickened from the dead;
> I gave, I gave My life for thee,
> What hast thou given for Me?
>
> My Father's house of light,
>   My glory-circled throne
> I left for earthly night,
>   And wanderings sad and lone;
> I left, I left it all for thee,
> Hast thou left aught for Me?

> I suffered much for thee,
>   More than thy tongue can tell,
> Of bitterest agony,
>   To rescue thee from hell;
> I've borne, I've borne it all for thee,
> What hast thou borne for Me?
>
> And I have brought to thee,
>   Down from My home above,
> Salvation full and free,
>   My pardon and My love;
> I bring, I bring rich gifts to thee,
> What hast thou brought to Me?

* * *

I KNOW THAT MY REDEEMER LIVES

CHARLES WESLEY'S HYMNS are the product of a sensitive, affectionate nature, an offset to the sterner make-up of his famous brother.

The gifted Charles wrote literally hundreds of hymns, many of which were unpublished. Many were revised by his brother John, and often cut down very considerably.

The famous *Foundry Collection* (1739) contained many of our best-loved hymns. Not only did the Wesleys bring out their own book—after forty-two years in the field—but they added new tunes to suit the hymns. These tunes were different from the Psalm tunes which were in use for the Wesleys fully realized the power of song upon the masses.

It was in 1759 that Charles adapted and rewrote the hymn below, from a poem of many stanzas.

The Wesley family believed in the supernatural world; when they were children at Epworth rectory, which was frequently visited by Poltergeist phenomena, the family was not afraid, but took the ghostly manifestations as a matter of course.

John Wesley frequently alluded to the spirit world in

his diary. "How often are spirits present when we do not think of it," he wrote. And again, "How hard it is to keep the middle way." In another entry he expressed himself in these words: "How strange is this! but how little we know concerning the laws of the invisible world."

Charles Wesley believed that God speaks to people through common things. To him the line between life and death scarcely existed.

This was probably due to the early teaching of his mother, Susannah Wesley. When she died the family stood round the bed and sang a hymn of praise that she was now with the saints.

Charles Wesley's voice has long been hushed, but he still pleads in his Master's cause; he still comforts those that mourn. His memorial rests securely in his hymns.

> I know that my Redeemer lives,
>   And ever prays for me;
> A token of His love He gives,
>   A pledge of liberty.
>
> I find Him lifting up my head;
>   He brings salvation near;
> His presence makes me free indeed,
>   And He will soon appear.
>
> He wills that I should holy be;
>   What can withstand His will?
> The counsel of His grace in me
>   He surely shall fulfill.
>
> When God is mine, and I am His,
>   Of Paradise possessed,
> I taste unutterable bliss
>   And everlasting rest.

*   *   *

I'M PRAYING FOR YOU

MR. SANKEY related in his *Reminiscence of Sacred Song* that on his first visit to Ireland in 1874, he came across these words printed on a little leaflet and signed "S. O'Maley Cluff."

"Moody was also taken with the words," he wrote, "so I set them to music. It was my second hymn composition."

On one occasion, a minister was asked to visit a sick man who was opposed to evangelism, but yet wanted the preacher to visit him. The visitor told afterward that he went into the room and, seeing a little organ in the corner, asked permission to sing. He sang these lines and then had a talk with the invalid, although he was careful not to intrude the subject of religion into the conversation. But the song had done its work in the man's heart.

Dwight L. Moody told many stories of the power given to this hymn.

He related that a young man from Sweden told him that he first heard this song in his native land. It was sung by two evangelists who went from house to house to hold a series of meetings. The two-roomed log house was packed and after one evangelist had prayed, the other said, "Sing one of Sankey's hymns."

The young man continued: "Since then I have heard this sweet hymn sung in many places. I have heard it in primitive homes on the Western prairies and by great choirs in our large cities. But whenever I do hear it I am a lad again in the little log home in Sweden."

> I have a Saviour, He's pleading in glory,
>   A dear, loving Saviour, tho' earth friends be few;
> And now He is watching in tenderness o'er me,
>   But oh, that my Saviour were your Saviour too!
>
> (Chorus)
> For you I am praying,
> For you I am praying,

For you I am praying,
I'm praying for you.

I have a Father, to me He has given
    A hope for eternity, blessed and true;
And soon He will call me to meet Him in heaven,
    But oh, that He'd let me bring you with me too.

I have a robe, 'tis resplendent in whiteness,
    Awaiting in glory my wondering view;
Oh, when I receive it all shining in brightness,
    Dear friend, could I see you receiving one too!

*   *   *

I MUST TELL JESUS*

ELISHA A. HOFFMAN was born at Orwigsburg, Pennsylvania, in 1839.

His father was a minister, so when Hoffman was a young man it was natural that he, too, should join in the work of the Gospel in the Evangelical Association. He said that his earliest recollection of Gospel hymns was his mother singing them at home.

He was a poet, musician and a prolific writer of both words and music of many revival hymns that swept America and other countries.

Hoffman, when pastor of a church at Lebanon Pennsylvania, had a peculiar experience which, he related, inspired him to write the following hymn.

"I called one day at the home of a parishioner and found the lady in great distress and sorrow," he said. "She was overwrought. Wringing her hands she cried, 'What shall I do; what shall I do?' I replied, 'You cannot do better than to take it all to Jesus—you must tell Jesus; you must tell Jesus.'

"For a moment she seemed absorbed with her thoughts and then her face glowed, her eyes lighted up, and with animation she exclaimed, 'Yes, I must tell Jesus; I must tell Jesus!'

"As I went from that sorrow-filled home I had a vision of a joy-illumined face, of a soul transformed from darkness into light, and I heard all along my pathway the echo of a tender voice saying 'I must tell Jesus.'

"Immediately on reaching my study I penned off the words, and before very long I had composed the melody to suit them."

> I must tell Jesus all of my trials;
>   I cannot bear my burdens alone;
> In my distress He kindly will help me;
>   He ever loves and cares for His own.
>
> (Chorus)
> I must tell Jesus! I must tell Jesus!
>   I cannot bear my burdens alone;
> I must tell Jesus! I must tell Jesus!
> Jesus can help me, Jesus alone.
>
> I must tell Jesus all of my troubles;
>   He is a kind, compassionate Friend;
> If I but ask Him, He will deliver,
>   Make of my troubles quickly an end.
>
> Tempted and tried I need a great Saviour,
>   One who can help my burdens to bear;
> I must tell Jesus! I must tell Jesus!
> He all my cares and sorrows will share.
>
> Oh, how the world to evil allures me!
>   Oh, how my heart is tempted to sin!
> I must tell Jesus, and He will help me,
>   Over the world the victory to win.

*   *   *

IN THE LAND OF STRANGERS

HORATIUS BONAR was still actively at work at the age of eighty. He always said that he had so much to do and the time was short.

This great Scottish hymn writer was also a writer of many tracts, one of which, "Believe and live" ran into ten thousand copies.

Bonar was physically and mentally a strong man. He was gifted with a voice loud enough to be clearly heard in a large crowd. Often he would preach several times on a Sunday, frequently to outdoor gatherings.

He was about sixty-three when Moody and Sankey first visited Scotland. Bonar wrote many hymns for these favorite evangelists, not the least of which was "I Was a Wandering Sheep." It is well known that Bonar's hymns were framed at odd times: sometimes in railway trains or when walking home under the stars, sometimes by the lonely seashore or near a bubbling brook which tumbled down some hillside.

At one time editor of the *Journal of Prophecy*, Horatius Bonar was much interested in biblical prophecies—those which had already been fulfilled, and those which had not yet come to pass. Thoughts of the Second Advent were often present in the mind of this saintly man and are evident in many of his hymns.

Bonar was a pioneer in the singing of hymns in the church. Many of his own beautiful hymns he never heard sung, for hymn singing at that time was an innovation. However, by the time Moody and Sankey left Scotland the people had been taught to love hymns.

Bonar's wife was the sister of Mrs. Duncan who wrote "Jesus, Tender Shepherd, Hear me" . . . and who died at the early age of twenty-five.

Bonar wrote this hymn in 1874, by special request of Ira D. Sankey.

In 1894 it was sung by a choir of fifteen hundred voices in the great Convention Hall in Washington and proved to be the favorite of the choristers.

> In the land of strangers,
>   Whither thou art gone,
> Hear a far voice calling,
>   "My son! my son!
>
> (Chorus)
> "Welcome, wanderer, welcome!
>   Welcome back to home!
> Thou hast wandered far away;
>   Come home, come home!
>
> "From the land of hunger,
>   Fainting, famished, lone,
> Come to love and gladness,
>   My son! my son!
>
> "Leave the haunts of riot,
>   Wasted, woebegone,
> Sick at heart and weary,
>   My son! my son!
>
> "See the door still open!
>   Thou art still my own;
> Eyes of love are on thee,
>   My son! my son!
>
> "Far off thou hast wandered;
>   Wilt thou farther roam?
> Come, and all is pardoned,
>   My son! my son!
>
> "See the well-spread table,
>   Unforgotten one!
> Here is rest and plenty,
>   My son! my son!"

*   *   *

I'VE FOUND A FRIEND

James Grindley Small, the author of the following hymn, was born at Edinburgh, Scotland, in 1817. When he was attending the University in his native city, he had the great fortune to meet Professor Chalmers, who made a lasting impression on his life . . . Chalmers was an influence for good to many young men.

After graduation, Small became a minister of the Free Church of Scotland at Bervie, near Montrose. He was a better writer than speaker; nevertheless, he was very much liked. He had a kindly and sympathetic disposition, and was a good listener.

At the University he won a prize for a poem, "The Highlands," and in honor of this award he named his first book, *The Highlands and Other Poems*. Several other books of poems followed. His book *Psalms and Sacred Songs*, 1866, was praised by the critics.

This hymn was first published in the *Revival Hymn Book*, 1863, and later on in other hymn books. It was soon set to music by the fine musician, Sir Joseph Barnby, and inserted in the *Scottish Hymn Book*. However, it was not until Sankey sang the wonderful words, that the hymn became known to the world. George C. Stebbins gave it the melody loved by all.

Ira D. Sankey related that he sang this hymn during a meeting in the north of England. There were several Quaker ladies in the audience. A written request to repeat the hymn the next evening was sent to Sankey by these ladies, although it was not their custom to ask anyone to sing.

> I've found a Friend, oh, such a Friend!
> He loved me ere I knew Him;
> He drew me with the cords of love,
> And thus He bound me to Him;

And 'round my heart still closely twine
  Those ties which naught can sever,
For I am His, and He is mine,
  Forever and forever.

I've found a Friend, oh, such a Friend!
  He bled, He died to save me;
And not alone the gift of life,
  But His own self He gave me.
Naught that I have mine own I'll call,
  I'll hold it for the Giver;
My heart, my strength, my life, my all,
  Are His, and His forever.

I've found a Friend, oh, such a Friend!
  All power to Him is given,
To guard me on my onward course,
  And bring me safe to heaven:
Eternal glory gleams afar,
  To nerve my faint endeavor:
So now to watch, to work, to war;
  And then to rest forever.

I've found a Friend, oh, such a Friend!
  So kind and true and tender!
So wise a Counsellor and Guide,
  So mighty a Defender!
From Him who loves me now so well
What power my soul shall sever?
Shall life or death, shall earth or hell?
  No: I am His forever.

* * *

JESUS IS TENDERLY CALLING

FANNY CROSBY, the blind poetess and writer of many hymns which were made famous the world over by numerous noted evangelists, related that it was her habit before she composed a hymn to sit for a while with an open New Testament before her. She would place both hands upon its pages, and the words then flowed easily to her lips, as though she were being directed what to say. All of her sacred poems were inspirations.

Fanny Crosby had many musical friends, who set her beautiful words to attractive and tuneful melodies which never failed to catch the listener's ear and to linger in his mind.

The musical Dr. H. Doane was always a kind and sympathetic friend. There were many others including Ira D. Sankey, George Stebbins, W. H. Bradbury, Dwight L. Moody, and H. P. Main, who set this particular hymn to a melody which he named after the first line of the hymn. These leaders in the evangelical world sang Fanny Crosby's sweet hymns into the hearts of the people.

It was an age of American hymn writers, including the talented sisters, Susanna and Anna Warner, who wrote the familiar "Jesus Loves Me," and "Jesus Bids Us Shine."

Fanny Crosby tersely says of her blindness: "I verily believe that it was God's intention that I should live my days in physical darkness so as to be better prepared to sing His praises and incite others so to do. I could not have written thousands of hymns if I had been hindered by the distractions that would have been presented to my notice."

Some of Fanny Crosby's hymns were written when she was well in her seventies. Age was no hindrance to her poetic gifts and it was said that she could still remember the words of most of the hymns she had written.

> Jesus is tenderly calling thee home—
>   Calling today, calling today;
> Why from the sunshine of love wilt thou roam,
>   Farther and farther away?
>
> (Chorus)
> Calling today!
> Calling today!
> Jesus is calling,
> Is tenderly calling today.

Jesus is calling the weary to rest—
  Calling today, calling today;
Bring Him thy burden, and thou shalt be blest;
  He will not turn thee away.

Jesus is waiting, oh, come to Him now—
  Waiting today, waiting today;
Come with thy sins, at His feet lowly bow;
  Come, and no longer delay.

Jesus is pleading, oh, list to His voice—
  Hear Him today, hear Him today;
They who believe on His Name shall rejoice,
  Quickly arise and away!

*   *   *

JESUS, KEEP ME NEAR THE CROSS

FANNY CROSBY lost her eyesight when only six weeks old. Educated at New York City Institute for the Blind, she seems to have been in happy surroundings. In 1858 she married a blind musician, Alexander van Alstyne, who eventually became a teacher in that institution.

There is a story that one New York firm requested her to write three hymns a week for a year, a contract which she performed to the letter and in addition supplied another firm with literally hundreds of hymns.

Fanny Crosby had such fluency of expression that peoms seemed to be on her lips at all times.

She wrote, too, for such gifted composers as Dr. Doane, Philip Phillips, Robert Lowry and Ira D. Sankey. She had a singular regard for Sankey, who appeared to her to be God's messenger of song. She had known him in the early years of his mission. Bradbury, too, and indeed all the musicians of sacred song of that day, set Fanny Crosby's beautiful words to haunting melodies that their hearers could not forget.

The charm and simplicity of the musical setting which Dr. Doane gave this hymn, made it a great favorite.

> Jesus, keep me near the Cross,
>   There a precious fountain
> Free to all—a healing stream,
>   Flows from Calvary's mountain.
>
> (Chorus)
> In the Cross, in the Cross,
>   Be my glory ever;
> Till my raptured soul shall find
>   Rest beyond the river.
>
> Near the Cross, a trembling soul,
>   Love and mercy found me;
> There the Bright and Morning Star
>   Sheds its beams around me.
>
> Near the Cross! O Lamb of God,
>   Brings its scenes before me;
> Help me walk from day to day,
>   With its shadows o'er me.
>
> Near the Cross I'll watch and wait,
>   Hoping, trusting ever,
> Till I reach the golden strand,
>   Just beyond the river.

* Copyright 1890 by W. H. Doane.

* * *

JESUS LOVES ME

ANNA WARNER, born in 1820 at Highland Falls, New York, was a year younger than her famous sister, Susan.

She was a novelist, too, and became popular in collaboration with Susan in a number of stories and novels. Anna had the pen name of Amy Lothrop.

Anna Warner was very fond of hymns. At thirty-eight she edited *Hymns of the Church Militant,* and ten years later *Wayfaring Hymns, Original and Translated.*

Susan Warner died at the age of sixty-four and Anna wrote her sister's biography, which was greatly valued.

This hymn, written by Anna and published in her *Original Hymns,* was sung by children everywhere, and it became a favorite in Sunday schools.

In the autumn of 1943, a young man who came into Winnipeg, Canada, from the far north to enlist in the army, told the writer the following story:

"Sometimes," said he, "I would accompany a French Canadian trapper on the round of his line. As our snowshoes went swiftly over the glistening whiteness, Pierre always sang the same song, sometimes in French, sometimes in Eskimo. I liked it, and asked him to teach me the words. He did, in the Eskimo language. I said, 'Where did you pick that up?' 'Oh,' he said, 'at the mission. ' "

And so this cheerful song by Anna Warner, and the tuneful melody of William B. Bradbury were often heard, when the air was crisp and still, over the ice and snow of the Arctic wastelands.

> Jesus loves me! this I know,
> For the Bible tells me so;
> Little ones to Him belong;
> They are weak, but He is strong.
>
> (Chorus)
> Yes, Jesus loves me!
> Yes, Jesus loves me!
> Yes, Jesus loves me!
> The Bible tells me so!
>
> Jesus loves me! loves me still,
> Tho' I'm very weak and ill;
> From His shining throne on high
> Comes to watch me where I lie.
>
> Jesus loves me! He who died,
> Heaven's gate to open wide;
> He will wash away my sin,
> Let His little child come in.

Jesus loves me! He will stay,
Close beside me all the way;
If I love Him when I die,
He will take me home on high.

*   *   *

JESUS OF NAZARETH PASSETH BY

TOWARD THE END of the year 1863, a remarkable religious revival took place in New York City.

A great awakening to spiritual things —after a lapse of many years—was shaking the foundations of that busy city. Hundreds of people were seen wending their way to the revival meetings at all hours of the day. People were seeking something, they knew not what.

At the meeting one afternoon was a Miss Emma Campbell, a poet and writer of songs. As she sat in the vast audience she was arrested by the text given out by the preacher, R. J. Pardee. It was from Luke 18:37, "They told him, that Jesus of Nazareth passeth by."

Miss Campbell saw how deeply the people were moved— as she was—and the whole scene remained firmly in her mind. When she reached the quiet of her home she wrote these moving lines.

Some time elapsed before T. E. Perkins composed the well-known tune which was made famous later on by Sankey. He used it at his first meeting in England, in 1873, and it proved to have a great appeal. Indeed, it is said that thousands of people changed their lives through the power given to this hymn.

Andrew Bonar, brother of the hymn writer, wrote about this in his *Life of James Scott.*

"Some of us listening," he wrote, "to these two messengers, Moody and Sankey (the one singing, the other preaching), used to think of what is told in IIKings 3:15. Elisha, before beginning to prophesy, called for a minstrel, and when the camp of soldiers had been calmed and melted by harp and song, the hand of the Lord came upon the preacher.

"Had you been in Edinburgh, Scotland, during the four months when these brethern were there in 1873, you would have seen multitudes of all ages and stations hastening to the place of meeting, at whatever hour and every day of the week. The scene was exactly that described in the hymn so often sung, and so much blessed."

What means this eager, anxious throng,
Which moves with busy haste along—
These wondrous gath'rings day by day?
What means this strange commotion, pray?
In accents hushed the throng reply:
"Jesus of Nazareth passeth by."

Who is this Jesus? Why should He
The city move so mightily?
A passing stranger, has He skill
To move the multitude at will?
Again the stirring notes reply:
"Jesus of Nazareth passeth by."

Jesus! 'tis He who once below
Man's pathway trod, mid pain and woe;
And burdened ones, where'er He came
Brought out their sick, and deaf, and lame;
The blind rejoiced to hear the cry:
"Jesus of Nazareth passeth by."

Again He comes! from place to place
His holy footprints we can trace
He passeth at our threshold—nay,
He enters—condescends to stay.
Shall we not gladly raise the cry—
"Jesus of Nazareth passeth by"?

Ho! all ye heavy-laden, come!
Here's pardon, comfort, rest, and home!
Ye wanderers from a Father's face!
Return, accept His proffered grace.
Ye tempted ones, there's refuge nigh:
"Jesus of Nazareth passeth by."

But if you still this call refuse,
And all His wondrous love abuse,
Soon will He sadly from you turn,
Your bitter prayer for pardon spurn.
"Too late! too late!" will be the cry—
"Jesus of Nazareth has passed by."

*   *   *

JESUS SAVES! JESUS SAVES!

WILLIAM J. KIRKPATRICK was a native Irishman, born in 1838, and like many others from the Emerald Isle, he inherited the gift of music and poetry.

When he was still a child, his parents immigrated to America and William lived for the rest of his life in the United States.

He served in the Civil War, as the leader of the fife band of the ninety-first Regiment of the Pennsylvania Volunteers. Afterward he was drafted to ship building. For some years following the end of hostilities he continued in commercial pursuits.

The time came when he had a sudden change of heart and decided to devote his life to God's service in the way he best knew—music.

He wrote many sacred songs, both words and music. He edited *Collections of Sacred Songs,* and became known far and wide through his compositions. Indeed, Sankey made good use of them in his first book of hymns. One in particular, "Jesus Saves," is still a great favorite with the Salvation Army.

This hymn owed a great deal to Kirkpatrick's music. The words were written by Priscilla J. Owens.

When William Kirkpatrick died in 1921, at the age of eighty-three, it is said that he was sitting in his chair writing a hymn on a sheet of paper which fluttered to the floor from his lifeless fingers.

We have heard the joyful sound:
  Jesus saves! Jesus saves!
Spread the tidings all around:
  Jesus saves! Jesus saves!
Bear the news to every land,
  Climb the steeps and cross the waves,
Onward, 'tis the Lord's command;
  Jesus saves! Jesus saves!

Waft it on the rolling tide:
  Jesus saves! Jesus saves!
Tell to sinners far and wide:
  Jesus saves! Jesus saves!
Sing, ye islands of the sea,
  Echo back, ye ocean caves,
Earth shall keep her jubilee;
  Jesus saves! Jesus saves!

Sing above the battle's strife:
  Jesus saves! Jesus saves!
By His death and endless life,
  Jesus saves! Jesus saves!
Sing it softly thro' the gloom,
  When the heart for mercy craves,
Sing in triumph o'er the tomb,
  Jesus saves! Jesus saves!

Give the winds a mighty voice:
  Jesus saves! Jesus saves!
Let the nations now rejoice,
  Jesus saves! Jesus saves!
Shout salvation, full and free,
  Highest hills and deepest caves,
This our song of victory,
  Jesus saves! Jesus saves!

*   *   *

JESUS, STILL LEAD ON

JANE LAURIE BORTHWICK was born at Edinburgh, in 1813.
Like her sister she soon discovered her own literary and
poetic gifts. Both began to publish works that arrested
attention.

Her sister married a minister of the Free Church of Scotland—Rev. Eric Findlayton—whose parsonage at Lochearnhead was set in unsurpassed scenic grandeur.

Jane Borthwick spent some part of her holidays each year on the continent. She and her sister were both fluent linguists; and they absorbed much of the literature of the countries they visited.

Shortly after she returned from one of her visits to Switzerland, Jane was reading some German translations to her father. He was so charmed that he persuaded her to translate a book of hymns. This was brought out in collaboration with her sister and entitled *Hymns from the Land of Luther.*

This hymn was one of those translated and is included in the *Scottish Hymn Book.* Its author was Von Zinzendorf.

Miss Borthwick was a devoted social worker in many activities of the Free Church of Scotland. One of her favorite interests was the Moravian Mission in Labrador.

Jane Borthwick lived to the ripe old age of eighty-four and to enjoy what is so often denied authors, the appreciation and success of her published works. She was laid to rest in Edinburgh, the home of her fathers.

> Jesus, still lead on,
> Till our rest be won;
> And although the way be cheerless,
> We will follow calm and fearless;
> Guide us by Thy hand
> To our Fatherland.
>
> If the way be drear,
> If the foe be near,
> Let not faithless fear o'ertake us,
> Let not faith and hope forsake us;
> For, through many a foe,
> To our home we go.
>
> When we seek relief
> From a long-felt grief,
> When temptations come, alluring,

Make us patient and enduring,
  Show us that bright shore,
  Where we weep no more.

Jesus, still lead on,
Till our rest be won;
Heavenly Leader, still direct us,
Still support, console, protect us,
  Till we safely stand
  In our Fatherland.

*   *   *

JESUS, THESE EYES HAVE NEVER SEEN

ALL THE WORLD knows the beautiful hymn, "My Faith Looks Up to Thee," which was composed by Ray Palmer at the age of twenty-one. Twenty-eight years afterward—when a new hymn book was being brought out—Dr. Palmer wrote the following hymn in response to a request for a contribution.

This is the story of the way the hymn came to be written.

One evening, Ray Palmer was sitting in his little study at home, preparing a sermon for the following Sunday.

His subject was "Faith in Christ." He turned to the first chapter of Peter's first Epistle and read: "That the trial of your faith, being much more precious than of gold that perisheth, though it be tried with fire, might be found unto praise and honour and glory at the appearing of Jesus Christ: whom having not seen, ye love; in whom, though now ye see him not, yet believing, ye rejoice with joy unspeakable and full of glory."

In relating the story, Dr. Palmer tells how the theme opened up to him.

"I needed a volume from my closed bookcase on the other side of the room. I rose from my chair and walked over to get it. As I opened the door, the very book appeared straight to my hand. At once it occurred to me that in some such way the face of Christ would be unveiled to us, and the thought so filled my heart that I turned to my desk and composed the hymn."

It is said that the words of the last stanza of this poem were on his lips just before he died.

>Jesus, these eyes have never seen
>   That radiant form of Thine!
>The veil of sense hangs dark between
>   Thy blessed face and mine.
>
>I see Thee not, I hear Thee not,
>   Yet art Thou oft with me;
>And earth has ne'er so dear a spot,
>   As where I meet with Thee.
>
>Like some bright dream that comes unsought,
>   When slumbers o'er me roll,
>Thine image ever fills my thought,
>   And charms my ravished soul.
>
>Yet though I have not seen, and still
>   Must rest in faith alone;
>I love Thee, dearest Lord!—and will,
>   Unseen, but not unknown.
>
>When death these mortal eyes shall seal,
>   And still this throbbing heart,
>The rending veil shall Thee reveal
>   All glorious as Thou art!

* * *

JOY TO THE WORLD

IT IS SAID that it was a remark made by his father that turned Isaac Watts to hymn writing.

One Sunday morning after returning from the church service, Isaac criticized a hymn that had been sung, whereupon his father remarked, "Well, you'd better try your own hand at writing one."

"I will, Father," he said, and not very long afterward wrote his first hymn, "Behold the Glories of the Lamb." It is in our hymnbooks today.

When a guest of his kind friends, Sir Thomas and Lady Abney—where he used often to stay—someone once remarked that Watts was quite small, and then another said "What! is this the great Dr. Watts!"

He replied immediately in a stanza from his lyrics:

> Were I so tall to reach the pole,
> Or grasp the ocean with a span,
> I must be measured by my soul,
> The mind's the standard of a man.

Watts was an artist as well as a poet. He found much pleasure within the beautiful grounds of his hosts and made marked strides toward becoming an acknowledged painter.

It was his custom to read in one of the sheltered nooks in the garden. One particular book was about the Esthonians and their legend of song.

The god of song, they said, descended on the land where there was a sacred wood, and there he played and sang.

Around him stood the creatures, and each learned its own portion of the celestial strain. The tree discovered how to rustle its leaves, the brook how to murmur along its bed, and the wind and the birds and the beasts alike caught the parts assigned to them.

Man only was able to combine these strains, and, therefore, man alone can rightly praise.

It was in this mood that he penned this hymn. Watts was then about forty-five.

> Joy to the world; the Lord is come!
> Let earth receive her King;
> Let every heart prepare Him room,
> And heaven and nature sing.
>
> Joy to the earth; the Saviour reigns;
> Let men their songs employ;

While fields and floods, rocks, hills and plains,
  Repeat the sounding joy.

No more let sins and sorrows grow,
  Nor thorns infest the ground;
He comes to make His blessings flow
  Far as the curse is found.

He rules the world with truth and grace,
  And makes the nations prove
The glories of His righteousness,
  And wonders of His love.

*   *   *

LET THE LOWER LIGHTS BE BURNING

THE SECRET of Dwight L. Moody's power was his earnestness; he believed it was God's purpose not only "to make men good but to make them good for something."

One evening P. P. Bliss had gone to hear the famous evangelist preach to a crowded hall.

As he told them about a shipwreck which had happened one very dark night, he held the rapt attention of his audience. This was the story.

Only one light was visible as a pilot strove against the tempest to guide the vessel to a safe harbor.

The captain was doubtful whether the pilot had rightly judged the position of the port, for other lights invisible to him ought to have marked hidden dangers. But the pilot was quite sure that he was right on his course.

The captain asked, "Where are the lower lights?"

"Gone out, sir."

"Can you make it?" asked the anxious captain.

"We must or we shall be lost, sir!"

The pilot did his best, but the storm was furious and without the guiding lights they struck a rock, and quickly the ship broke up. Many passengers were drowned in the wild seas.

At this point in the story, Moody roused his audience with these ringing words, "Brothers, the Master will take care of the great lighthouse. Let us keep the lower lights burning!"

P. P. Bliss could not forget this illustration. He soon scribbled down the words of this hymn, which seemed to come straight from his heart.

> Brightly beams our Father's mercy
> From His lighthouse evermore,
> But to us He gives the keeping
> Of the lights along the shore.
>
> (Chorus)
> Let the lower lights be burning!
> Send a gleam across the wave!
> Some poor fainting, struggling seaman
> You may rescue, you may save.
>
> Dark the night of sin has settled,
> Loud the angry billows roar;
> Eager eyes are watching, longing,
> For the lights along the shore.
>
> Trim your feeble lamp, my brother;
> Some poor sailor, tempest-tossed,
> Trying now to make the harbor,
> In the darkness may be lost.

*   *   *

LIKE SILVER LAMPS IN A DISTANT SHRINE

IT WAS IN THE YEAR 1837 that Dr. Dix of Bristol welcomed a son whom he named William Chatterton. Little did the father think at the time that this same son would be famous for his many beautiful hymns.

William Dix was brought up within sight of the sea. His home was but a short walk from the busy docks of this prominent seafaring town. Here ships from every corner of the world glided into port.

The Dix family were a jolly household. The mother was musical and many happy hours were spent around the piano in music and song. William's poems were set to tunes by his mother and sung on Sunday evenings.

The Dix family inherited literary tastes, for the boy's grandfather had written a biography of the Bristol poet Chatterton, after whom William was named.

He was educated at the Bristol Grammar School where lessons on marine insurance were included. He entered a marine insurance company and later became manager of a firm at Glasgow.

William Dix had a delicate constitution. He was frequently at home sick, sometimes for quite a long period. It was on one of these occasions, while convalescent, that most of his hymns were written.

It was during the Christmas season of 1867, after reading the account of the Nativity in Luke 2:7, "She . . . wrapped him in swaddling clothes, and laid him in a manger," that his poet's spirit was inspired to write the following beautiful Christmas Carol.

> Like silver lamps in a distant shrine,
>   The stars are sparkling bright;
> The bells of the city of God ring out
>   For the Son of Mary is born tonight.
> The gloom is past, and the morn at last
>   Is coming with orient light.
>
> No earthly songs are half so sweet
>   As those which are filling the skies,
> And never a palace shone half so fair
>   As the manger-bed where our Saviour lies;
> No night in the year is half so dear
>   As this which has ended our sighs.
>
> The stars of heaven still shine as at first
>   They gleamed on this wonderful night;
> The bells of the city of God peal out,

And the angels' song still rings in the height,
And love still turns where the Godhead burns,
  Hid in Flesh from fleshly sight.

Faith sees no longer the stable floor,
  The pavement of sapphire is there,
The clear light of heaven streams out to the world,
  And angels of God are crowding the air,
And heaven and earth, through the spotless birth,
  Are at peace on this night so fair.

*   *   *

MASTER, THE TEMPEST IS RAGING

MISS MARY BAKER was a writer of songs, both sacred and secular.

She had a dearly loved brother who for reasons of health had to seek southern warmth as the chill of winter approached. At this particular time her brother was in the south, but he had become very ill. Mary herself was sick in bed and quite unable to travel.

During this sad and anxious time of waiting, her brother died and Mary lost faith in God and for a time was very unhappy. As time passed, she recovered somewhat from her apathy. Then one day there reached her a request to write some hymns suitable for the Sunday school *Series of Lessons* which were about to be drawn up. The subject was "Christ and the Tempest."

Mary Baker felt that she herself had been shaken to the depths by a terrible tempest. The theme seemed to be part of her own experience.

The words of the first stanza tell of Christ stilling the tempest; the second, of the anguish of her own soul; the third, of her return to the trust and security of God's goodness and of her deep contrition for her doubts and fears.

The author had this to say about it: "I supposed that the

hymn had done its work and gone to rest. But during the
weeks when our nation kept watch by the bedside of our
greatly beloved President Garfield, the hymn was repub-
lished as especially appropriate to the time, and was sung
at some of the many funeral services held throughout the
United States. It was quite a surprise to me that this hymn
should have crossed the seas and been sung in far distant
lands to the honor of the Saviour's Name."

The attractive melody was composed by H. R. Palmer.

> Master, the tempest is raging!
>   The billows are tossing high!
> The sky is o'er shadowed with blackness
>   No shelter or help is nigh:
> Carest Thou not that we perish?
>   How canst Thou lie asleep,
> When each moment so madly is threat'ning
>   A grave in the angry deep?
>
> (Chorus)
> The winds and the waves shall obey Thy will,
> Peace . . . be still! . . .
> Whether the wrath of the storm-tossed sea
>   Or demons or men, or whatever it be,
>   No waters can swallow the ship where lies
>   The Master of ocean, and earth, and skies:
>   They all shall sweetly obey Thy will,
>   Peace, be still! Peace be still!
>   They all shall sweetly obey Thy will,
>   Peace, peace, be still!
>
> Master, with anguish of spirit
>   I bow in my grief today;
> The depths of my sad heart are troubled—
>   Oh, waken and save, I pray!
> Torrents of sin and of anguish
>   Sweep o'er my sinking soul;
> And I perish! I perish! dear Master—
>   Oh, hasten, and take control.
>
> Master, the terror is over,
>   The elements sweetly rest;
> Earth's sun in the calm lake is mirrored,
>   And heaven's within my breast;

Linger, O blessed Redeemer!
Leave me alone no more;
And with joy I shall make the blest harbor,
And rest on the blissful shore.

* Copyright 1941. Hope Publishing Company, owner.

* * *

MORE HOLINESS GIVE ME

PHILIP BLISS was born in Clearfield County, Pennsylvania, in 1838. In later years he changed his name and signed himself Philip P. Bliss.

When twelve years of age he was baptized into the Baptist communion of Cheery Flats, Tioga County, Pennsylvania. However, the revival services at the Methodist church, where he had many friends, held a great interest for him. Bliss there came in touch with William B. Bradbury, the famous singer of sacred songs. Together they formed a singing team which attracted thousands of people to revival services.

When twenty-six years of age, Bliss joined George F. Root, another evangelists, in Chicago. They toured the western states together and attended various musical conventions.

Dwight L. Moody met Bliss when he was thirty-four and at once claimed him for service.

The world soon knew of the wonderful revival meetings held by Moody and Sankey, and of the beautiful voices of Bliss and Whittle.

Philip Bliss was the happy possessor of a most charming voice, sympathetic and appealing, for singing was to him the language of the heart. Audiences everywhere were greatly attracted by his personality. The following hymn, thrilling in its earnestness, is from his pen.

But a tragic end awaited this favored man. He and his

wife were on their way by rail to Chicago. It was December 29, 1867. During the journey Bliss was busy studying his Bible and putting down notes for a new song he was writing. Suddenly at Ashtabula, Ohio, a bridge gave way and the train was plunged into the shallow stream below. The cars caught fire. Bliss escaped through a window, but when he could not find his wife, returned to save her. They both perished in the flames.

> More holiness give me, more strivings within;
> More patience in suffering, more sorrow for sin;
> More faith in my Saviour, more sense of His care;
> More joy in His service, more purpose in prayer.
>
> More gratitude give me, more trust in the Lord;
> More pride in His glory, more hope in His Word
> More tears for His sorrows, more pain at His grief;
> More meekness in trial, more praise for relief.
>
> More purity give me, more strength to o'ercome;
> More freedom from earth-stains, more longings for home;
> More fit for the kingdom, more used would I be,
> More blessed and holy, more, Saviour, like Thee.

*   *   *

NOTHING BUT LEAVES

In 1874 at Providence, Rhode Island, Lucy Eveline Akerman died at the early age of twenty-four. "But she having lived for so short a time had fulfilled a long time," and was the author of a hymn which in the words of Ira D. Sankey "was of great use in the Master's service."

Sankey said that he sang the hymn as a solo at many of his first meetings, especially when Dwight L. Moody was to speak on "The Holy Spirit."

"At a meeting in Birmingham, England," he related, "I was singing it and a lady in the audience came to me afterward and declared that she intended to devote the rest of her life to Christ. Others also began a new life, for such was the powerful message that the words contained that it turned thoughts and hearts to service."

This hymn beautifully expresses the meaning of the parable of the fig tree. In Matthew 21:18-20 we find these words: "Now in the morning as he returned into the city, he hungered. And when he saw a fig tree in the way, he came to it, and found nothing thereon, but leaves only, and said unto it, Let no fruit grow on thee henceforward for ever. And presently the fig tree withered away."

Dr. Whedon explains this was an incident of the second day of Passion Week. Our Lord probably left Bethlehem before His breakfast that He might attend the morning service at the Temple.

The parable of the fig tree is symbolical of the Messiah's peace to the Gentiles. The fig tree promised fair, but it was like the Jewish nation, it had no fruit; its withering under His malediction was the perdition of the Jewish State and System.

The Jewish nation had the leaves of a favored nation above all nations, or better, alone of the nations; but it was like them, barren. It had no business to be putting forth leaves and so pretending to have fruit, like a hypocrite with a fair show of profession without any meaning.

Moody and Sankey considered this hymn the expression of a leading evangelistic truth.

> Nothing but leaves! The Spirit grieves
>   O'er years of wasted life;
> O'er sins indulged while conscience slept,
> O'er vows and promises unkept,
>   And reap from years of strife—
> Nothing but leaves! Nothing but leaves!
>
> Nothing but leaves! No gathered sheaves
>   Of life's fair ripening grain;
> We sow our seeds; lo! tares and weeds—

Words, idle words, for earnest deeds—
    Then reap, with toil and pain,
Nothing but leaves! Nothing but leaves!

Nothing but leaves! Sad memory weaves
    No veil to hide the past;
And as we trace our weary way,
And count each lost and misspent day,
    We sadly find at last—
Nothing but leaves! Nothing but leaves!

*   *   *

OH, FOR A FAITH

WILLIAM HILEY BATHURST was born in 1796 at the famous
beauty spot, Clive Dale, near Bristol, England.

His father was known far and wide as Charles Bragg,
member of Parliament for Bristol. At the death of his
uncle, his father took the name of Bathurst when he succeeded as next-of-kin to the family estate of which beautiful Sydney Park, Gloucestershire, was the seat.

William went to Winchester College, thence to Christ
Church, Oxford. On graduation in 1818, he entered the
church.

William Bathurst was afflicted with extreme shyness.
He shunned busy cities and towns and was appointed to
a country parish outside the big city of Leeds, where he
stayed for thirty-three years.

His parishioners came to love their quiet, sincere, earnest
vicar, for he never spared himself or his substance in their
behalf. At the age of fifty-five Bathurst resigned his
living, and went to live in the lovely surroundings of
Matlock, Derbyshire, devoting himself to literary pursuits.

It was when he was at the parish near Leeds that he
wrote the following hymn and published his *Psalms and
Hymns for Public and Private use.*

William Bathurst died at the age of eighty-one.

Oh, for a faith that will not shrink
   Though pressed by every foe,
That will not tremble on the brink
   Of any earthly woe;

That will not murmur nor complain
   Beneath the chastening rod,
But in the hour of grief or pain,
   Will lean upon its God;

A faith that shines more bright and clear
   When tempests rage without,
That when in danger knows no fear,
   In darkness feels no doubt;

A faith that keeps the narrow way
   Till life's last hour is fled,
And with a pure and heavenly ray
   Lights up a dying bed.

Lord! give us such a faith as this,
   And then, whate'er may come,
We'll taste ev'n here the hallowed bliss
   Of an eternal home.

*   *   *

O MASTER, LET ME WALK WITH THEE

Washington Gladden was born at Potts Grove, Pennsylvania, in 1836. He decided, when quite a young lad, to become a minister of the Gospel. He entered Williams College, and at the age of twenty-four was ordained into the Congregational ministry. He served churches at Brooklyn, New York; Morrisania, New York; and finally Columbia, Ohio, where he stayed for over thirty-four years. He died there at the age of eighty-two.

During the course of a long career he was well known in journalistic circles; indeed, he was known to his day and generation as a writer on many subjects. He was greatly interested in civic affairs and wrote various articles for the betterment of social service.

Gladden himself told how he wrote the poem which unexpectedly turned into this hymn. "This hymn," he related, was written for "The Still Hour" a corner in *Sunday Afternoon,* a paper which was filled with good reading. In March, 1879, it was published in three eight-line stanzas. The lines unsuitable for worship were left out and the poem became a hymn. The poem was not written for a hymn; it was my friend, Rev. C. H. Richards, who saw in the lines their suitability and adapted it so."

> O Master, let me walk with Thee
> In lowly paths of service free;
> Tell me Thy secret; help me bear
> The strain of toil, the fret of care.
>
> Help me the slow of heart to move
> By some clear winning word of love;
> Teach me the wayward feet to stay,
> And guide them in the homeward way.
>
> Teach me Thy patience! still with Thee
> In closer, dearer company,
> In work that keeps faith sweet and strong,
> In trust that triumphs over wrong,
>
> In hope that sends a shining ray
> Far down the future's broadening way;
> In peace that only Thou canst give,
> With Thee, O Master, let me live!

*   *   *

ON CHRIST, THE SOLID ROCK, I STAND

EDWARD MOTE was born in London in 1797. As a young man he was in business in the city.

At that time he had not intended to enter the ministry. However, largely influenced by the preaching of Rev. J.

Hyatt, of the Tottenham Court Road Baptist Chapel, Mote decided to enter the Baptist ministry.

He served different communities during the succeeding few years; then when about fifty years old, he took charge of the Baptist congregation at Horsham, Sussex. Here he stayed until his death twenty-six years later.

Edward Mote related the following story: "One morning it came into my mind as I went to labor, to write a hymn on 'The Gracious Experience of a Christian.' As I went up Holborn I had the chorus. During the day I had four stanzas complete, and wrote them off. On the Sabbath following I met brother King as I came out of Lisle street meeting, who informed me that his wife was very ill, and asked me to call and see her.

"I had an early tea, and called afterward. He said it was his usual custom to sing a hymn, read a portion and engage in prayer before he went to the meeting. He looked for his hymnbook, but could not find it anywhere. I said I had some stanzas of a hymn in my pocket; if he liked we would sing them. We did; and his wife enjoyed them so much that, after service, he asked me, as a favor, to leave a copy of them for her. I went home, and by the fireside composed the last two stanzas, wrote the whole off, and took them to sister King.

"As this hymn so met the dying woman's case, my attention to it was the more arrested, and I had a thousand copies printed for distribution. I sent one to *Spiritual Magazine,* without my initials, and it appeared in due course."

In the author's *Hymns of Praise* (1836) there were six stanzas. These were cut down to the four now to be found in many hymn books.

Bishop Bickersteth, who wrote "Peace, Perfect Peace," maintained that this was a great hymn of faith.

My hope is built on nothing less
Than Jesus' blood and righteousness;
I dare not trust the sweetest frame,
But wholly lean on Jesus' name:

(Chorus)
On Christ, the solid rock, I stand;
All other ground is sinking sand,
All other ground is sinking sand.

When darkness veils His lovely face,
I rest on His unchanging grace;
In every high and stormy gale,
My anchor holds within the veil:

His oath, His covenant, His blood,
Support me in the whelming flood;
When all around my soul gives way,
He then is all my hope and stay:

When He shall come with trumpet sound,
Oh, may I then in Him be found,
Dressed in His righteousness alone,
Faultless to stand before the Throne!

*   *   *

ONE MORE DAY'S WORK FOR JESUS

DWIGHT L. MOODY, and Ira D. Sankey were men who filled
the religious need of the hour. They spoke the language of
the people. No one could estimate the good that these
missionaries accomplished by the singing of hymns. They
knew how to impress their words on an audience—how to
spread a rich banquet.

Sankey told a story of fresh young voices of children
singing this hymn. The words floated through the open
window of a mission chapel, and a woman who was passing
stopped to listen. She told afterward that she went home
with these words fixed in her mind.

The next day was washday, and as she was bending over

the washtub, the haunting words of the hymn came again into her mind. She suddenly began to think about their meaning, and she said to herself: "Have I ever done one day's work for Jesus in my life? No, I have not. But I will from now on."

This was the beginning of a new life for the hard-worked mother. She told them at the mission that from then on she had had a new outlook—she washed the clothes for Jesus, cleaned the house for Jesus, looked after the family for Jesus.

A strong light and a pulsing life had come, and had worked a miracle. At the end of the day she could sing with a different feeling and fresh enthusiasm, "One more day's work for Jesus."

This is one of the hymns of Anna Warner, the celebrated American hymn writer, who wrote many hymns especially for children.

> One more day's work for Jesus,
>   One less of life for me!
> But heav'n is nearer,
> And Christ is dearer,
>   Than yesterday to me;
> His love and light
> Fill all my soul tonight.
>
> (Chorus)
> One more day's work for Jesus,
> One more day's work for Jesus,
> One more day's work for Jesus,
> One less of life for me.
>
> One more day's work for Jesus;
>   How glorious is my King!
> 'Tis joy, not duty,
> To speak His beauty,
>   My soul mounts on the wing
> At the mere thought
> How Christ my life has bought.

One more day's work for Jesus;
　　How sweet the work has been,
To tell the story,
To show the glory,
　　Where Christ's flock enter in!
How it did shine
In this poor heart of mine.

One more day's work for Jesus—
　　Oh, yes, a weary day;
　But heav'n shines clearer,
And rest comes nearer,
　　At each step of the way;
And Christ in all—
Before His face I fall.

Oh, blessed work for Jesus!
　　Oh, rest at Jesus' feet!
There toil seems pleasure,
My wants are treasure,
　And pain for Him is sweet,
Lord, if I may,
I'll serve another day.

*　　*　　*

PASS IT ON

HENRY BURTON was a Britisher. When a little child he
was taken by his parents to the United States, and was
brought up there. He was graduated from Beloit College
and was ordained into the Methodist Episcopal church.

On his return to his native England at Swannington,
Leicestershire, he was at once given a charge in Lancashire.
Later he worked in London.

Henry Burton was a writer of poetry as well as an author
of prose. He had a number of books to his credit, not to
mention many articles on various subjects.

His book of poems, *Wayside Songs,* had a wide circulation, but of all of his writings his two hymns are the ones best remembered.

The hymn given here was written at Acton, London, on April 8, 1885, when he was forty-five. It was first printed in *The Christian Advocate,* New York, in 1886.

The author said the hymn was based on a little incident in the life of his brother-in-law, Rev. Guy Pearse. When he was a boy returning home from a Moravian school in Holland, the steward of the boat on which he sailed from Bristol to Hayle showed him marked attention and kindness, because Mr. Pearse's father, years before, had proved a great friend to the steward's mother. And so this man was simply passing on the kindness.

> Have you had a kindness shown?
> Pass it on!
> 'Twas not given for thee alone;
> Pass it on!
> Let it travel down the years,
> Let it wipe another's tears,
> Till in heaven the deed appears—
> Pass it on!
>
> Did you hear the loving word?
> Pass it on!
> Like the singing of a bird—
> Pass it on!
> Let its music live and grow,
> Let it cheer another's woe;
> You have reaped what others sow—
> Pass it on!
>
> 'Twas the sunshine of a smile—
> Pass it on!
> Staying but a little while!
> Pass it on!
> April beam, the little thing,
> Still it wakes the flowers of spring,
> Makes the silent birds to sing—
> Pass it on!

Have you found the heavenly light?
    Pass it on!
Souls are groping in the night,
    Daylight gone:
Hold thy lighted lamp on high,
Be a star in someone's sky;
He may live who else would die—
    Pass it on!

Be not selfish in thy greed—
    Pass it on!
Look upon thy brother's need—
    Pass it on!
Live for self, you live in vain;
Live for Christ, you live again;
Live for Him, with Him you reign—
    Pass it on!

PASS ME NOT

IF WE KNEW the inner life of many of the people we work with and do business with and meet socially, we would feel more kindly toward them. Grief makes life hard for many people, but there is always comfort for those who turn to Christ, even though they mourn.

This was the keynote of the much loved blind poetess, Fanny Crosby, who received various inspirations for the writing of her hymns. Her's was an age of evangelistic singing missions, and Fanny Crosby's hymns were always in request. So popular was the little poetess that she was invited to speak at many places where these missions were held.

On one occasion, it was at a state prison. Much was hoped for from this particular meeting. As Fanny was speaking— and her very blindness gave her power—first one prisoner and then another would interrupt by calling on the good Lord "not to pass me by."

Fanny told that she was so touched by the pleas of these

men that she could not get the thought of them out of her mind; indeed she said, "I wrote the lines with the men's pleading wail still in my ears."

And so it was that Fanny Crosby, who dwelt less in a world of persons and places than in a realm of ideas, came to write this hymn that is known everywhere.

> Pass me not, O gentle Saviour,
>   Hear my humble cry;
> While on others Thou art calling
>   Do not pass me by.
>
> (Chorus)
> Saviour, Saviour,
>   Hear my humble cry;
> While on others Thou art calling,
>   Do not pass me by.
>
> Let me at a throne of mercy
>   Find a sweet relief;
> Kneeling there in deep contrition,
>   Help my unbelief.
>
> Trusting only in Thy merit,
>   Would I seek Thy face;
> Heal my wounded, broken spirit,
>   Save me by Thy grace.
>
> Thou the Spring of all my comfort,
>   More than life to me;
> Whom have I on earth beside Thee?
>   Whom in heaven but Thee?

* * *

RESCUE THE PERISHING

MANY OF Fanny Crosby's hymns were favorites of the evangelists, Moody and Sankey. Not a campaign was concluded without the hymns of the inspired blind poetess being used extensively. Ira D. Sankey could tell many a tale of the miraculous haunting power these hymns had over people—the words seemed to recall to them their spiritual destination.

One cold winter's day a miserable middle-aged man stumbled into a mission in the slums of New York during the singing of this hymn. Stupefied with liquor, unkempt and unwashed, he huddled into a corner.

The hymn woke a dormant chord in his memory; then his dulled reason slowly returned. When the preacher mentioned the soldiers in the Civil War, the poor outcast shed tears. He, too, had been in that War.

Now thoroughly aroused, he arose and going close to the preacher said, "When were you in that company you spoke of?"

"Why, all through the war," said the preacher "Do you remember the battle of . . ."

"Perfectly!"

"Do you remember the name of the captain of your company at that time?"

The preacher mentioned the name of the captain.

"Yes," said the ragged man, "I am he! Look at me—everything has left me through drink! The hymn you have just sung speaks to me of hope, even for a wretch like me!"

The preacher was used to outcasts; he helped to restore that unfortunate man's self-respect, and in course of time he was able to fill something of his old position in the world . . . saved from the depths through a hymn!

The hymn was written as a battle cry for church workers everywhere and Moody and Sankey knew how to use it with great effect.

Dr. Doane composed the music—which arrested the passer-by. He was honored by Dennison University with the degree of Doctor of Music for his work in sacred song.

> Rescue the perishing, care for the dying,
>   Snatch them in pity from sin and the grave;
> Weep o'er the erring one, lift up the fallen,
>   Tell them of Jesus the mighty to save.

(Chorus)
Rescue the perishing, care for the dying;
Jesus is merciful, Jesus will save.

Though they are slighting Him, still He is waiting,
    Waiting the penitent child to receive;
Plead with them earnestly, plead with them gently;
    He will forgive if they only believe.

Down in the human heart, crushed by the tempter,
    Feelings lie buried that grace can restore;
Touched by a loving hand, wakened by kindness,
    Chords that were broken will vibrate once more.

Rescue the perishing, duty demands it;
    Strength for thy labor the Lord will provide;
Back to the narrow way patiently win them;
    Tell the poor wanderer a Saviour has died.

*   *   *

RING THE BELLS OF HEAVEN

IT WAS AMERICA who gave the world many of our Gospel
songs. Hymns and sacred songs have been a tremendous
influence in all denominations.

George F. Root, whose numerous attractive words and
tunes are in most hymnbooks, left a request that when he
died only the Doxology was to be sung at his funeral.

Born in 1820, at Sheffield, Massachusetts, Root was to be
a power for good in the musical world of his day. Cushing,
Root, Bradbury, Mason—and other sweet singers of the age
—made a memorable time for the United States.

They discovered that hymns do help. No one can reckon
the blessings that these talented and inspired men bestowed
on mankind. They knew that hymns have a way of remain-
ing in the heart. They fasten upon the imagination and
become nourishment for the mind as well as manna for
the soul.

Root was famous as a conductor of choral societies. He soon joined his friend Lowell Mason and taught in schools. Children everywhere loved the tuneful melodies that Root composed for them to sing. He wished to inspire people to love service for the Master, and he did this with his songs.

We know how scenes of long ago are brought back to us by the scent of a flower—so is memory refreshed by hymns. Many a man on the battlefield recalls his childhood days— especially when he is in danger. Words that are sung are close to the heart and take us into another world.

Ira D. Sankey made good use of the following hymn in his many evangelistic services in all countries.

> Ring the bells of heaven! there is joy today,
>   For a soul, returning from the wild;
> See! the Father meets him out upon the way,
>   Welcoming His weary wand'ring child.
>
> (Chorus)
> Glory! glory! how the angels sing;
> Glory! glory! how the loud harps ring;
> 'Tis the ransomed army, like a mighty sea,
> Pealing forth the anthem of the free.
>
> Ring the bells of heaven! there is joy today,
>   For the wand'rer now is reconciled;
> Yes, a soul is rescued from his sinful way,
>   And is born anew a ransomed child.
>
> Ring the bells of heaven! spread the feast today,
>   Angels, swell the glad triumphant strain!
> Tell the joyful tidings! bear it far away!
>   For a precious soul is born again.

* * *

SAVIOUR, LIKE A SHEPHERD LEAD US

DOROTHY ANN THRUPP was born in London, in 1779.

Not very much is known of her childhood, but we find her as a young woman engaged in literary pursuits, contributing poems and hymns to various small magazines suitable for children.

In the first years of the nineteenth century Dorothy was known as a writer for young people.

It was the fashion of the time to circulate publications among the various infant schools of the country. It was also an age of impending change. Dorothy Thrupp entered upon life as great efforts were being made for the betterment of mankind.

James Watt, a Scottish engineer, inventor of the steam engine, was having a struggle to secure a patent for his invention. The unfortunate George III was on the throne and was striving against adversities without and within. William Wilberforce was toiling to abolish slavery. As a young woman Dorothy Thrupp saw England turned into an armed camp against the threatened French invasion.

Dorothy was a little girl of nine when the beloved Charles Wesley died. She probably remembered John Wesley, for he died two years later.

At fifty years of age Dorothy Thrupp brought out a book of hymns and poems for the young. Several of the hymns are in various collections today. "A Widowed Mother Lost Her Son" is still in use, and the better known "A Little Ship Was on the Sea" is a favorite of many. The following hymn is known to all.

> Saviour, like a shepherd lead us,
>   Much we need Thy tend'rest care;
> In Thy pleasant pastures feed us,
>   For our use Thy folds prepare;
> Blessed Jesus, blessed Jesus,
>   Thou hast bought us, Thine we are;
> Blessed Jesus, blessed Jesus,
>   Thou hast bought us, Thine we are.
>
> We are Thine; do Thou befriend us,
>   Be the Guardian of our way;
> Keep Thy flock, from sin defend us,
>   Seek us when we go astray;

Blessed Jesus, blessed Jesus,
  Hear, oh, hear us when we pray;
Blessed Jesus, blessed Jesus,
  Hear, oh, hear us when we pray.

Thou hast promised to receive us,
  Poor and sinful though we be;
Thou hast mercy to relieve us,
  Grace to cleanse, and power to free;
Blessed Jesus, blessed Jesus,
  Let us early turn to Thee;
Blessed Jesus, blessed Jesus,
  Let us early turn to Thee.

Early let us seek Thy favor,
  Early let us do Thy will;
Blessed Lord and only Saviour
  With Thy love our bosoms fill;
Blessed Jesus, blessed Jesus,
  Thou hast loved us, love us still;
Blessed Jesus, blessed Jesus,
  Thou hast loved us , love us still.

*   *   *

SAVIOUR, SPRINKLE MANY NATIONS

Arthur Cleveland Coxe was born at Mendham, New Jersey, in 1818. He was a son of the manse, his father being a minister in a Presbyterian church in Brooklyn.

Young Coxe attended the University of New York. He was graduated in 1841 and was ordained into the Episcopal church. In due course he became rector of St. John's in Hartford, Connecticut.

Within the next twenty years or more, Coxe served churches in Baltimore and Calvary Church, New York City, where he was greatly esteemed. In 1865 he was chosen Bishop of Western New York.

Not only in church circles was Arthur Coxe highly regarded, but the field of poetry and literature also claimed him. He published several books, one entitled *Impressions of England* which was written after a visit to that lovely country in 1865. Then followed *Sermons on Doctrine and Duty*. He also contributed to newspapers, magazines and other publications. His name signed to any article assured it wide attention by the public.

But of all his literary works, this hymn will perhaps be the most lasting. It was written for the use of missions in his own Diocese of Western New York.

Arthur Coxe believed in the religion of love, that "if we love one another, God dwelleth in us."

Saviour, sprinkle many nations,
  Fruitful let Thy sorrows be;
By Thy pains and consolations,
  Draw the Gentiles unto Thee;
Be it to the nations told;
  Of Thy Cross the wondrous story,
Let them see Thee in Thy glory
  And Thy mercy manifold.

Far and wide, though all unknowing,
  Pants for Thee each mortal breast;
Human tears for Thee are flowing,
  Human hearts in Thee would rest;
Thirsting, as for dews of even,
  As the new-mown grass for rain,
Thee they seek, as God of heaven,
  Thee, as Man for sinners slain.

Saviour, lo, the isles are waiting,
  Stretched the hand, and strained the sight,
For Thy Spirit new creating,
  Love's pure flame and wisdom's light;
Give the word, and of the preacher,
  Speed the foot and touch the tongue,
Till on earth by every creature,
  Glory to the Lamb be sung.

*   *   *

SOLDIERS OF CHRIST, ARISE

PEOPLE TODAY cannot realize how much John and Charles Wesley suffered from persecution in the first years of their ministry. But Methodism was gradually to live down persecution and win the hearts of the people.

John joined his brother at Nottingham one October day in 1743. He had come from Wednesbury, some distance away, and his clothes were torn to tatters. A mob from three towns had dragged him about for several hours, determined to murder him, but he had been wonderfully delivered by a man who had snatched him from the crowd and had swum across the river with him on his back.

On another occasion a Quaker came to the rescue of Charles by lending him his broadbrimmed hat, which may have saved his life.

Charles urged his people to suffer all things patiently and to ask God for direction where to preach.

At St. Ives, in Cornwall, about the year 1744, Charles Wesley told Henry Moore that after hearing himself abused longer than usual in a sermon at church, he stayed to the Sacrament. The minister, who noticed him waiting in his pew, called to his clerk and they conversed some time within the Communion rail. The service then proceeded.

When Charles Wesley approached, the clergyman retreated toward the wall, and the clerk advanced holding out the large prayer book, and crying, "Avaunt, Satan! Avaunt!" Charles remained for sometime; but nothing would quiet the clerk, and so he retired to his pew and the service went on.

Charles Wesley was also refused the Sacrament at the Temple Church, in London.

But Cornwall was won for Methodism. The miners had learned to sing the Wesleys' hymns, among them this one by Charles.

Soldiers of Christ, arise,
  And put your armour on,
Strong in the strength which God supplies
  Through his eternal Son.

Strong in the Lord of hosts,
  And in His mighty power,
Who in the strength of Jesus trusts,
  Is more than conqueror.

Stand, then, in His great might,
  With all His strength endued,
And take, to arm you for the fight,
  The panoply of God;—

From strength to strength go on,
  Wrestle and fight and pray;
Tread all the powers of darkness down,
  And win the well-fought day!

That, having all things done,
  And all your conflicts past,
Ye may o'ercome through Christ alone,
  And stand entire at last.

Jesus, Eternal Son,
  We praise Thee and adore,
Who art with God the Father One
  And Spirit evermore.

*   *   *

SWEET HOUR OF PRAYER

WILLIAM BRADBURY was a piano maker. He was born in New York, Maine, in 1816.

From the very beginning of his life the world of music beckoned, but he was poor and his health was not robust. However, after a time William obtained the assistance of Lowell Mason, who most generously took upon himself the lad's musical education.

William Bradbury lived for a few years at St. John, New

Brunswick, Canada. Later he became organist of a Baptist
church at Brooklyn; also at Maine, Boston. In a few years
we find him at the Baptist Tabernacle in New York City
where he made a name for himself among children by teaching them singing. In fact he has been called "The father of
Sunday school music." Bradbury was in great request as a
teacher and organized musical festivals for juveniles.

After a year spent in Europe for educational purposes, he
returned home and immediately set about organizing Sunday school singing. He gave the young voices simple tunes
which they could easily remember. It was an age when
there were very few children's hymns, and it was in children that William was chiefly interested.

In the world of music he was a success. Many of the older
generation may have heard his cantata, *Esther,* which had a
tremendous vogue in its day. He was editor of many music
books.

He was in ill health as he grew into middle age, and for
some years before he died, at the age of fifty-two, he suffered from lingering tuberculosis.

This particular hymn was written by W. W. Walford,
a songwriter of that day, but it was the tune composed by
Bradbury that made the hymn known. Another hymn made
famous by his composition was Anna Bartlett Warner's
"Jesus Loves Me."

> Sweet hour of prayer! sweet hour of prayer!
> That calls me from a world of care,
> And bids me at my Father's throne
> Make all my wants and wishes known;
> In seasons of distress and grief,
> My soul has often found relief,
> And oft escaped the tempter's snare,
> By thy return, sweet hour of prayer!
>
> Sweet hour of prayer! sweet hour of prayer!
> Thy wings shall my petition bear
> To Him whose truth and faithfulness
> Engage the waiting soul to bless.

And since He bids me seek His face,
Believe His Word, and trust His grace
I'll cast on Him my every care,
And wait for thee, sweet hour of prayer!

Sweet hour of prayer! sweet hour of prayer!
May I thy consolation share,
Till, from Mount Pisgah's lofty height,
I view my home and take my flight;
This robe of flesh I'll drop and rise
To seize the everlasting prize;
And shout while passing through the air,
Farewell, farewell, sweet hour of prayer!

*   *   *

TAKE ME AS I AM

IT IS OFTEN said that memory is the highest gift. We remember the past that has formed us into our present selves, and a song may awaken within us thoughts that lie too deep for tears. This is very often true of a hymn as it wings its magic way to an appointed task.

Mr. Moody has told many human and touching stories of his life's work. Here is one:

"One day," he related, "a gentleman called at my office, bringing with him a young man who had just been released from prison. The man held back, not liking to enter, but I said, 'Bring him in.'

"I took him by the hand, told him I was glad to see him, and invited him to my home.

"In due course the young man called, and I introduced him to my family. When my little daughter came into the room I said, 'Emma, this is papa's friend,' and she went up to him and kissed him.

"The man could not control his emotions; he covered his

face with his hands and wept. When she left the room I said, 'What is the matter?'

" 'Oh, sir,' was the reply, 'I have not had anyone to treat me like that since my mother died. I thought that never again would I find a friend.'

"At that moment there came from the next room the strains of music. It sounded in his ears like the voice of an angel, for it was to him like healing balm for the wounds of life.

"He fell on his knees and sought for peace. . . as the words of the hymn were clearly heard."

How the words came to be written is told in the following story:

Before the time of the great revivalists, Moody and Sankey, a revival was taking place in a certain part of Scotland.

In the mission hall was a poor servant girl who became greatly distressed about herself as she listened to the preacher. On the way home, weeping bitterly, she called at the manse to consult the minister as to "how to be changed."

"Oh," said he, "say your prayers and read your Bible and you'll be safe enough."

"O, mister," she cried, "I canna read, I canna pray," and throwing herself on her knees with uplifted eyes she pathetically implored, "Lord Jesus, tak' me as I am! Oh, tak' me as I am."

Someone related this story to the song writer, Eliza H. Hamilton, who was inspired to write this hymn. Sankey soon set the words to music, and the hymn became a wonderful power for good.

> Jesus, my Lord, to Thee I cry,
> Unless Thou help me, I must die;
> Oh, bring Thy free salvation nigh,
>   And take me as I am!
>
>   ‧ (Chorus)
>   Take me as I am,
>   Take me as I am;

Oh, bring Thy free salvation nigh,
And take me as I am!

Helpless I am, and full of guilt,
But yet Thy blood for me was spilt,
And Thou cans't make me what Thou wilt,
And take me as I am!

No preparation can I make,
My best resolves I only break,
Yet save me for Thine own Name's sake,
And take me as I am!

Behold me, Saviour, at Thy feet,
Deal with me as Thou seest meet;
Thy work begin, Thy work complete,
And take me as I am!

*　　*　　*

TELL ME THE OLD, OLD STORY

KATHERINE HANKEY was born at Clapham, London, England, in 1834.

Her father was an evangelical of the old school, and so it was natural that his daughter Kate, as she was known, took an active part in teaching in the Sunday school of the Clapham Sect.

Her father was very well off, being connected with the banking firm of the same name. He gave liberally to everything that furthered the cause of this particular evangelical sect.

Katherine had a large Bible class of girls before she was twenty. So interested was she in each member that more than fifty years afterward, many former pupils came long distances to her funeral.

The hymn given is an extract from a long poem of over fifty stanzas, written in two parts. The author herself gave the following account of the writing of the hymn:

"I wrote the first part toward the end of January, 1866. I was unwell at the time, just recovering from a severe illness, and the first stanza really indicates my state of health, for I was literally 'weak and weary.' When I had written the first part, which consisted of eight stanzas of four lines each, I laid it aside, and it was not until the following November that I completed the whole hymn."

This hymn, with its winning appeal, has been translated into almost every language under the sun. It gained great popularity from Dr. Doane's tune and from its frequent use by Ira D. Sankey, who sent it forth on its great mission.

How the talented Dr. Doane came to write the tune is an interesting story.

"In 1867," he related, "I was attending the International Convention of the Young Men's Christian Association, in Montreal. Among those present was Major General Russell, then in command of the English forces during the Fenian excitement. He arose in the meeting and recited the words of this song from a sheet of foolscap paper; tears streamed down his bronzed cheeks as he read. I wrote the music for the song one hot afternoon while on the stagecoach between the Glen Falls House and the Crawford House in the White Mountains.

"That evening we sang it in the parlor of the hotel. We thought it pretty, although we scarcely anticipated the popularity which was subsequently accorded it."

> Tell me the old, old story
>   Of unseen things above,
> Of Jesus and His glory,
>   Of Jesus and His love.
> Tell me the story simply,
>   As to a little child,
> For I am weak and weary,
>   And helpless and defiled.
>
> (Chorus)
> Tell me the old, old story,
> Tell me the old, old story,

Tell me the old, old story,
Of Jesus and His love.

Tell me the story slowly,
That I may take it in—
That wonderful redemption,
God's remedy for sin.
Tell me the story often,
For I forget so soon;
The "early dew" of morning
Has passed away at noon.

Tell me the story softly,
With earnest tones and grave;
Remember! I'm the sinner
Whom Jesus came to save.
Tell me the story always,
If you would really be,
In any time of trouble,
A comforter to me.

Tell me the same old story,
When you have cause to fear
That this world's empty glory
Is costing me too dear.
Yes, and when that world's glory
Is dawning on my soul,
Tell me the old, old story,
"Christ Jesus makes thee whole."

* * *

TELL MOTHER I'LL BE THERE

HERE IS an old-fashioned hymn that once was in vogue at
revival meetings.

Mr. Charles Alexander related that a friend of his cut
the poem out of a magazine and sent it to him. He kept it
and made a practice of always carrying it with him to his
evangelistic services.

One night in Newton, Kansas, Mr. Alexander was to sing
a solo. "I saw in the audience," he said, "a great crowd of

railway men, and with some doubt I finally decided to try this touching song, and was surprised at the extraordinary result.

"Many of the men stood up to join the forces of Christ. When the meeting was over, one big burly engineer came up to me and said 'Mr. Alexander, I promised my mother on her deathbed that I would become a Christian, but instead of that I have been going to the devil faster than ever. Preaching never touched me, but that song did.'

"I used that song every night, and have been using it ever since. I have seen as many as a hundred or a hundred and fifty men at a single meeting rise and confess Christ during the singing of that hymn before the sermon began. It reaches all classes, because everyone has a mother."

How it came to be written is a curious story. It was the time when President McKinley was in the White House. His mother lay dying in Ohio. Word was sent to him that his mother would like to see him before she died. The President had a special train prepared, and telegraphed "Tell Mother I'll be there."

> When I was but a little child how well I recollect
> How I would grieve my mother with my folly and neglect;
> And now that she has gone to heaven I miss her tender care:
> O Saviour, tell my mother I'll be there.
>
> (Chorus)
> Tell mother I'll be there, in answer to her pray'r,
> This message, blessed Saviour, to her bear!
> Tell mother I'll be there, heaven's joys with her to share,
> Yes, tell my darling mother I'll be there.
>
> Though I was often wayward, she was always kind and good;
> So patient, gentle, loving, when I acted rough and rude;
> My childhood griefs and trials she would gladly with me share:
> O Saviour, tell my mother I'll be there.
>
> When I became a prodigal, and left the old roof tree,
> She almost broke her loving heart in mourning after me;
> And day and night she prayed to God to keep me in His care:
> O Saviour, tell my mother I'll be there.

One day a message came to me, it bade me quickly come
If I would see my mother ere the Saviour took her home;
I promised her before she died, for heaven to prepare;
O Saviour, tell my mother I'll be there.

*   *   *

THE LIGHT OF THE WORLD IS JESUS

How OFTEN have congregations been carried away on the
waves of sacred song! Perhaps it was by a familar tune
known to them long ago. Preachers have frequently admit-
ted that more good has been done by sacred songs than by
sermons.

The popular "Singing Pilgrim," as Philip Bliss came
to be called, was well known on both sides of the Atlantic,
for Ira D. Sankey sang his appealing songs into the hearts
of the people.

The great revival held in England and Scotland by Moody
and Sankey, in 1873, owed much if its success to the pleas-
ing hymns and tunes introduced there for the first time.
Many of these were composed by Bliss, and, somehow,
people who heard them could not shake them off. Indeed, it
was as though the world was enveloped in sacred song.

Philip Paul Bliss was only thirty-eight years old when
he lost his life in a train accident while on his way to join
Sankey in Chicago. He died trying to save his wife from
a burning railway car. The world was much the poorer
for his passing.

To Bliss, the writing of music and song bearing a Gospel
message would so fill his heart with joy that the feeling
ran into the melody—and thence into hearts.

It was not for nothing that Philip Bliss was born in the
vast region of northern Pennsylvania. The very wildness and
softness of nature spoke to his inmost being. He grew up

listening to the music of the universe and when he was old enough to pluck the reeds he played the melodies he had learned.

The following hymn by Bliss, written for a revival meeting and sung by Ira D. Sankey, proved a favorite.

> The whole world was lost in the darkness of sin,
>   The Light of the world is Jesus;
> Like sunshine at noonday His glory shone in
>   The Light of the world is Jesus.
>
> (Chorus)
> Come to the Light, 'tis shining for thee;
> Sweetly the Light has dawned upon me,
> Once I was blind, but now I can see:
>   The Light of the world is Jesus.
>
> No darkness have we who in Jesus abide,
>   The Light of the world is Jesus;
> We walk in the Light when we follow our Guide,
>   The Light of the world is Jesus.
>
> Ye dwellers in darkness with sin-blinded eyes,
>   The Light of the world is Jesus;
> Go, wash at His bidding, and light will arise,
>   The Light of the world is Jesus.
>
> No need of the sunlight in heaven, we're told,
>   The Light of the world is Jesus;
> The Lamb is the light in the City of Gold,
>   The Light of the world is Jesus.

*   *   *

THE MORNING BRIGHT

THOMAS OSMOND SUMMERS was a native of Dorsetshire, England, where he was born in 1812.

His home was within a short distance of the historic ruin of Corfe Castle. This once grim castle was there in Edward the First's reign; indeed, a legend persists in the locality that the ghost of the martyred King Edward the Confessor haunts the site.

Now all is peaceful and on many a lovely day the only sounds are the sea waves lapping on the pebbled beach. It was in this quiet country that young Summers spent his youth.

The Summers' family were Nonconformists of the old strict school. Thomas was ordained into the same sect. At the age of twenty-eight he was at Baltimore, Maryland, and was working in a Methodist Episcopal church. He served there for five years, then went on to missionary work in Texas.

Summers was very interested in hymnology and was on the book committee of the Methodist Episcopal church. He worked hard to weed from the new hymnbook—of which he was editor—any songs which he considered inappropriate. He wished to dignify the hymnbook.

We find him next as Professor of Systematic Theology in Vanderbilt University, Nashville, Tennessee.

The hymn given was a general favorite with young people and was written for his own little daughter at the time Summers edited *Songs of Zion* in 1851.

> The morning bright with rosy light
>   Has waked me up from sleep;
> Father, I own Thy love alone
>   Thy little one doth keep.
>
> All through the day I humbly pray,
>   Be Thou my Guard and Guide;
> My sins forgive, and let me live
>   Blest Jesus, near Thy side.
>
> Oh, make Thy rest within my breast,
>   Great Spirit of all grace;
> Make me like Thee: then shall I be
>   Prepared to see Thy face.

*   *   *

THE NINETY AND NINE

GOSSAMER THREADS are so fine that they can scarcely be seen. Yet a web can be very strong for then one silken cord is linked to another.

So in the following story thin threads are woven into coincidence.

In Fergus, Ontario, Canada, lies the body of the man for whom was written the hymn "The Ninety and Nine." On his tombstone in St. Andrew's Presbyterian churchyard, Fergus is written:

> In memory of
> George,
> Eldest son of
> Andrew Clephane Esq.
> Late sheriff of
> Fifeshire, Scotland.
> A.D. 2 May, 1851
> Age 32.

Young Clephane, who was known as a remittance man, came to Canada to try farming about the year 1842. He was a fine young fellow, six feet or more tall, and made a number of friends in Fergus, who maintained that the young man was not cut out for rough work. His efforts at farming were not a success, a failure which led to indulgence in strong drink. The habit grew with his despondency, and during one of these bouts, while living with a medical doctor friend at Fergus, he died.

His sister Elizabeth had her brother in mind when she penned these now famous lines which were not in print until after her death. They were written in 1869, first published in *The Children's Hour* and thence copied in various magazines.

It was Mr. Sankey who saw the poem in a magazine, cut it out and put it in his note case.

At an evangelistic meeting in Edinburgh, in 1874, a sister of George and Elizabeth Clephane happened to be in the

audience when Moody—after his talk on the Good Shepherd—remarked to Sankey, "Sing something appropriate,
Sankey."

Sankey said he prayed for a tune. The answer came as he
put his hands on the organ keys, and sang for the first time
the tender lines of the hymn penned by a sister for her
brother in far-away Canada.

> There were ninety and nine that safely lay
>   In the shelter of the fold,
> But one was out on the hills away,
>   Far off from the gates of gold—
> Away on the mountains wild and bare,
> Away from the tender Shepherd's care.
>
> "Lord, Thou hast here Thy ninety and nine,
>   Are they not enough for Thee?"
> But the Shepherd made answer, "This of mine
>   Has wandered away from Me;
> And, although the road be rough and steep
> I go to the desert to find My sheep."
>
> But all thro' the mountains, thunder-riven,
>   And up from the rocky steep,
> There rose a cry to the gate of heaven,
>   "Rejoice! I have found My sheep!"
> And the angels echoed around the throne,
> "Rejoice, for the Lord brings back His own!"
>
> "They were shed for one who had gone astray,
>   Ere the Shepherd could bring him back."
> "Lord, whence are Thy hands so rent and torn?"
> "They are pierced tonight by many a thorn."
> "Lord, whence are those blood-drops all the way,
>   That mark out the mountain's track?"
>
> But none of the ransomed ever knew
>   How deep were the waters crossed;
> Nor how dark was the night that the Lord passed thro'
>   Ere He found His sheep that was lost.
> Out in the desert He heard its cry—
> Sick and helpless and ready to die.

*   *   *

THE SON OF GOD GOES FORTH TO WAR

BISHOP HEBER did much to make the singing of hymns popular in churches, for he believed in hymns as a powerful force for goodness, kindness and honest living.

Poetry came easily to his lips. As a student at Oxford he was the fortunate winner of the coveted Newdigate Prize for the best poem of the year.

One of his friends was Sir Walter Scott. Many pleasant times they had together when Scott entertained his friends at his home, Abbotsford. In Lord Tweedsmuir's *Memory Hold the Door* he referred to the room at Brasenose College, Oxford, where Heber entertained Scott.

Before Heber accepted the bishopric of Calcutta he had made plans to bring out a book of hymns. He hoped that Scott would be a contributor. However, the Bishop's Missionary work in India seems to have prevented it, but the wish to bring out a new book of hymns was very near to his heart.

During the last years of Bishop Heber's life—he lived only four years in India—the good bishop on several occasions made mention of Charles Wesley's hymns. He loved and had grown up under the tradition of that time and to him the words of the hymns were always precious.

A friend in India, who was with Heber often, commented of his love of a well-known hymn of Charles Wesley's, "Jesus, Lover of My Soul." He said that, in spite of one or two expressions, he admired this hymn as one of the most beautiful in our language for rich devotional feeling.

It was in far-away India, too, that Bishop Heber had one of the greatest pleasures of his poetic life. He wrote home in 1824, "I spent Christmas Day at Meerut, where on December 19 I dedicated a church. At this service I had the pleasure of hearing the hymn for St. Stephen's Day, "The Son of

God Goes Forth to War," sung better than I had ever
heard it before."

After the Bishop's death—in India, the result of a sun-
stroke—his wife brought out a collection of his fine hymns.

The Son of God goes forth to war,
    A kingly crown to gain;
His blood-red banner streams afar:
    Who follows in His train?
Who best can drink his cup of woe,
    Triumphant over pain,
Who patient bears his cross below—
    He follows in His train.

The martyr first, whose eagle eye
    Could pierce beyond the grave,
Who saw his Master in the sky,
    And called on Him to save:
Like Him, with pardon on his tongue,
    In midst of mortal pain,
He prayed for them that did the wrong:
    Who follows in his train?

A glorious band, the chosen few,
    On whom the Spirit came:
Twelve valiant saints, their hope they knew,
    And mocked the cross and flame.
They met the tyrant's brandished steel,
    The lion's gory mane;
They bowed their necks the stroke to feel:
    Who follows in their train?

A noble army, men and boys,
    The matron and the maid,
Around the Saviour's throne rejoice,
    In robes of light arrayed:
They climbed the steep ascent of heaven
    Through peril, toil and pain:
O God, to us may grace be given
    To follow in their train.

*   *   *

THOU ART GONE TO THE GRAVE

BISHOP HEBER wrote a number of very beautiful hymns. All the world knows his majestic "Holy, Holy, Holy, Lord God Almighty," and the great mission hymn, "From Greenlands Icy Mountains," which he wrote for his father-in-law, Dean Shipley, who was in urgent need of a mission hymn for the Sunday special mission service.

The young vicar of Hodnet, Heber, who was also lord of the manor of Hodnet in Shropshire, often drove his wife over to her old home at Wrexham rectory, and it was on one of these occasions that his famous hymn was written at the an hour's notice after dinner.

The brilliant young Heber had always a tender feeling for children. He was a good father. He had known deep sorrow in the loss of his beloved child.

When she died he wrote: "I am myself more cut down than I thought I should be, but I hope not impatient. I do not forget that to have possessed her at all, and to have enjoyed the pleasure of looking at her and caressing her was God's free gift, and still less do I forget that He who has taken her will at length, I hope, restore her to us."

This hymn was written during the time of mourning.

Reginald Heber had the true missionary spirit which urged him ever forward in the interests of the kingdom of heaven and he worked without sparing himself.

> Thou art gone to the grave, but we will not deplore thee,
>   Though sorrows and darkness encompass the tomb;
> The Saviour has passed through its portal before thee,
>   And the lamp of His love is thy guide through the gloom.
>
> Thou art gone to the grave, we no longer behold thee,
>   Nor tread the rough path of the world by thy side;
> But the wide arms of mercy are spread to enfold thee,
>   And sinners may hope, since the Sinless has died.
>
> Thou art gone to the grave, and, its mansion forsaking,
>   Perhaps thy tried Spirit in doubt lingered long;

But the sunshine of heaven beamed bright on thy waking,
   And the song which thou heard'st was the seraphims' song.

Thou art gone to the grave, but 'twere wrong to deplore thee,
   When God was thy ransom, thy guardian, thy guide;
He gave thee, and took thee, and soon will restore thee,
   Where death hath no sting, since the Saviour hath died.

*   *   *

'TIS SO SWEET TO TRUST IN JESUS

IT IS SAID that literally thousands of songs came from the hand of William J. Kirkpatrick. His Gospel songs were widely used in mission services.

Not only was he known and recognized as a composer of merit but he edited many collections of sacred songs and was one of the group of founders of American Gospel hymnody.

Ira D. Sankey, the man of the golden voice, sang Kirkpatrick's songs on all occasions.

So many of these sweet singers of America served their early careers in Sunday schools, and many tuneful melodies sung first by children's voices were thus introduced into general use.

Kirkpatrick's hymns are his monument. Who does not remember among many, "Jesus Saves!" "He Hideth My Soul" and "Coming Home"?

The words of this hymn, written by Louisa M. R. Stead, so appealed to the music-loving Kirkpatrick, that he set them to the melody that everyone knows.

James Kirkpatrick died very suddenly in his eighty-third year while engaged in writing a hymn. On the paper that fell to the floor, were these words in faint pencil:

> Just as Thou wilt, Lord, this is my cry;
> Just as Thou wilt to live or to die.

The summons had come.

> 'Tis so sweet to trust in Jesus,
> Just to take Him at His word;
> Just to rest upon His promise;
> Just to know, "Thus saith the Lord."
>
> (Chorus)
> Jesus, Jesus, how I trust Him,
> How I've proved Him o'er and o'er;
> Jesus, Jesus, precious Jesus!
> Oh, for grace to trust Him more.
>
> Oh, how sweet to trust in Jesus,
> Just to trust His cleansing blood;
> Just in simple faith to plunge me
> 'Neath the healing, cleansing flood.
>
> Yes, 'tis sweet to trust in Jesus,
> Just from sin and self to cease;
> Just from Jesus simply taking
> Life and rest and joy and peace.
>
> I'm so glad I learned to trust Thee,
> Precious Jesus, Saviour, Friend;
> And I know that Thou art near me,
> Wilt be with me to the end.

* * *

TRUE-HEARTED, WHOLE-HEARTED*

FRANCES RIDLEY HAVERGAL was born with a great poetic gift. From her early teens she showed unusual merit in verse composition. The family circle came to look upon its youngest member as a prodigy. Frances, unhappily, was always delicate; nevertheless, she accomplished much during her forty-three years of life.

Her father, who was rector of various churches, was very musical. He composed the tune "Patmos" for his daughter's hymn, "Take My Life and Let It Be." Frances stipulated that it was both her wish and that of her family that this tune should be the setting in all publications containing this hymn.

Frances apparently wrote her hymns quite spontaneously. For instance, when her father was rector of St. Nicholas' Church, Worcester, she and her sister were sleeping in the same room, when the pealing of the New Year's bells aroused them. Frances found a pencil and wrote a hymn commencing "As thy days, thy strength shall be." This hymn is in some of the hymnbooks today.

All Frances Ridley Havergal's hymns were inspirations. As a voice speaking from the soul, she poured forth her words. Each season of the Church's calendar, as it came round, she used as an opportunity to employ her gifts in the service of Him whom she delighted to call Master.

Frances Havergal meant people to sing as Paul wrote in his First Letter to the Corinthians: "I will sing with the spirit, and I will sing with the understanding also."

The melody to this hymn was composed by that master of song, George C. Stebbins, who belonged to the famous band of nineteenth century American evangelists.

> True-hearted, whole-hearted, faithful and loyal,
>   King of our lives, by Thy grace we will be;
> Under the standard exalted and royal,
>   Strong in Thy strength we will battle for Thee,
>
> (Chorus)
> Peal out the watchword! silence it never!
>   Song of our spirits, rejoicing and free;
> Peal out the watchword! loyal forever!
>   King of our lives, by Thy grace we will be.
>
> True-hearted, whole-hearted, fullest allegiance
>   Yielding henceforth to our glorious King;
> Valiant endeavor and loving obedience,
>   Freely and joyously now would we bring.

True-hearted, whole-hearted, Saviour all-glorious!
Take Thy great power and reign there alone,
Over our wills and affections victorious,
Freely surrendered and wholly Thine own.

*   *   *

WE WOULD SEE JESUS

ANNA WARNER, born at Highland Falls, New York, was the
gifted author of this wonderful hymn. Her sister Susan
wrote hymns, also. It was quite unique to have two such
talented sisters in one family. Both Susan and Anna wrote
hymns which will outlast the popular novel of that day
which Susan wrote and entitled *The Wide, Wide World.*

The day that adversity knocked at the Warners' door
fortune was dogging its footsteps, for it was not until their
father lost his income that the girls thought of working and
then they did not know what they could do to bring in
some money.

They were deeply religious and, believing that a way
would be opened, they began to write children's Bible
stories which they cleverly illustrated. These became very
much in demand. Anna and Susan succeeded, not without
many setbacks, but at last hard work brought its usual reward, and the home was saved.

All of their books had a distinctly religious tone. Anna
had more to do with hymns and hymn writing than her
sister, although Susan's "Jesus Bids Us Shine" is known
and loved by all.

Anna lived to the great age of ninety-five, and by remarkable coincidence was the exact contemporary of another loved hymn writer, Fanny Crosby who was also born
in 1820 and died in 1915.

We would see Jesus—for the shadows lengthen
  Across this little landscape of our life;
We would see Jesus, our weak faith to strengthen
  For the last weariness—the final strife.

We would see Jesus—other lights are paling,
  Whereon our feet were set with sovereign grace;
Not life, nor death, with all their agitation,
  Can thence remove us, if we see His face.

We would see Jesus—other lights are paling,
  Which for long years we have rejoiced to see;
The blessings of our pilgrimage are failing,
  We would not mourn them, for we go to Thee.

We would see Jesus—yet the spirit lingers
  Round the dear objects it has loved so long,
And earth from earth can scarce unclasp its fingers
  Our love to Thee makes not this love less strong.

We would see Jesus—sense is all too binding,
  And heaven appears too dim, too far away
We would see Thee, Thyself our hearts reminding
  What Thou has suffered, our great debts to pay.

We would see Jesus—this is all we're needing,
  Strength, joy and willingness come with the sight;
We would see Jesus, dying, risen, pleading,
  Then welcome, day, and farewell, mortal night!

*   *   *

WHAT A WONDERFUL SAVIOUR!

IN THE EARLY DAYS of Gospel singing the name of Elisha Hoffman was known far and wide. He was born at Orwigsburg, Pennsylvania, in 1839, and was a son of a minister of the Gospel of the Evangelical Association.

Elisha Hoffman was so musical that in his own words, "The hymns and tunes just bubbled from my heart to my lips." The poet-musician wrote many hymns and tunes which were used at revival meetings. Among them are the

familiar "What a Wonderful Saviour," "The Hour of Prayer"
and one that was used by the Salvation Army, "Whoever
Receiveth the Crucified One."

These once widely-known hymns may bring back to the
older generation memories of the past, for hymns sung in
early years haunt us as we grow older.

In World War I a soldier was brought into a clearing
station in France from No Man's Land, where he had been
lying for many hours. He was desperately wounded, but
after many weeks in the hospital he was on the mend and
on the following day was to be sent to the base hospital.

Before he left, a nurse said to him, "Weren't you afraid,
being alone in No Man's Land all those hours? What did
you think of while you were waiting to be brought in?"

"Oh," he replied, "I was not a bit afraid, for the most
lovely hymns kept floating through my mind—hymns that
I had forgotten long ago. They were messengers from
heaven sent to comfort and cheer me while I was lying
there!"

The power of sacred song had done its work. The melodies had entered the heart to stay; dire need had turned
them into "angels' voices."

> Christ has for sin atonement made,
>   What a wonderful Saviour!
> We are redeemed! the price is paid!
>   What a wonderful Saviour!
>
> (Chorus)
> What a wonderful Saviour is Jesus, my Jesus!
> What a wonderful Saviour is Jesus, my Lord!
>
> I praise Him for the cleansing blood,
>   What a wonderful Saviour!
> That reconciled my soul to God;
>   What a wonderful Saviour!
>
> He cleansed my heart from all its sin,
>   What a wonderful Saviour!
> And now He reigns and rules therein;
>   What a wonderful Saviour!

He gives me overcoming power,
  What a wonderful Saviour!
And triumph in each trying hour;
  What a wonderful Saviour!

To Him I've given all my heart,
  What a wonderful Saviour!
The world shall never share a part;
  What a wonderful Saviour!

*   *   *

WHEN THE ROLL IS CALLED UP YONDER*

AN EVANGELIST WORKER, J. M. Black, musician and poet, is the author of a little book of sacred poems, *Songs of the Soul*. He has told the story of the way he came to write the following hymn, which is contained in the volume and is often used at revival meetings.

Black related: "I saw a little girl sitting on the doorstep of a dilapidated house. Her worn clothes and dejected appearance told the story of a drunken father and mother and a miserable home.

"I spoke to the little girl and asked her if she would like to come to Sunday school. At the question, a wistful expression crept into the child's eyes and she softly answered, 'Yes, I would like to go but . . .'

"I understood what the little one meant, so I got together a surprise parcel containing a new dress, shoes and hat. Bessie was at Sunday school the next Sunday, and for many Sundays after.

"Then one Sunday when the roll call was called, no one answered to 'Bessie.' We called the name again, but there was no response.

"I found out that the little girl was very ill. The thought came to me in a flash, 'What if this little girl should die? What would her answer be when the final summons came?'

"Almost unconsciously I found myself saying the words, 'When the trumpet of the Lord shall sound, and time shall be no more.'

"No sooner had I written the rest of the words that evening than I went to the piano and struck off the music spontaneously. In a remarkably short time the hymn was finished and has been changed very little since that night."

When the trumpet of the Lord shall sound, and time shall be no more,
    And the morning breaks, eternal, bright and fair;
When the saved of earth shall gather over on the other shore,
    And the roll is called up yonder, I'll be there.

    When the roll is called up yonder,
    When the roll is called up yonder,
    When the roll is called up yonder,
    When the roll is called up yonder,
        I'll be there.

On that bright and cloudless morning when the dead in Christ shall rise,
    And the glory of His resurrection share;
When His chosen ones shall gather to their home beyond the skies,
    And the roll is called up yonder, I'll be there.

Let us labor for the Master from the dawn till setting sun,
    Let us talk of all His wondrous love and care;
Then, when all of life is over, and our work on earth is done,
    And the roll is called up yonder, we'll be there.

* Note: In "Hymns of the Christian Life" (Christian Publications, Inc.). Copyright 1921. Renewal by James H. Black. Hope Publishing Company, owner. Used by permission.

* * *

WHY DO YOU WAIT?

THE USE OF Psalms and hymns and spiritual songs has been part of the service of the Church down the ages. We read of the early Christians singing praises even in the arena as they awaited wild beasts. In later times sacred songs were made famous by singing evangelists on both sides of the water.

George Frederick Root, author of this hymn, was born at Sheffield, Massachusetts in 1820. He was an organist, conductor of various choirs, teacher and music publisher.

His songs were numerous and were sung and whistled everywhere—songs like "Tramp, Tramp, Tramp, the Boys Are Marching," and "Just Before the Battle Mother." Perhaps his hymn best known to Sunday schools was "When He Cometh." His cantatas had an extaordinary vogue, and his songs were sung by the soldiers in the American Civil War.

For fifteen years Root was organist in a Presbyterian church. He was only twenty-four when he traveled to New York and secured a post as teacher of voice production in Union Theological Seminary, and gave organ lessons as well.

America was fortunate in having such musical song writers as George Root and Lowell Mason, and his lifetime friend.

It was said of Root, that at the age of thirteen, he could play as many instruments as the years of his life.

Chicago University honored George Root with a Doctor's Degree of Music in recognition of his musical talents and as America's foremost writer of war songs.

A kindly personality . . . inspiring in his hymns . . . a man of high ideals . . . having served his day and generation, he fell asleep in 1895, aged seventy-five years.

> Why do you wait, dear brother,
>   Oh, why do you tarry so long?
> Your Saviour is waiting to give you
>   A place in His sanctified throng.
>
> (Chorus)
> Why not? why not?
> Why not come to Him now?
>
> What do you hope, dear brother,
>   To gain by a further delay?

There's no one to save you but Jesus,
    There's no other way but His way.

Do you not feel, dear brother,
    His Spirit now striving within?
Oh, why not accept His salvation,
    And throw off your burden of sin?

Why do you wait, dear brother?
    The harvest is passing away,
Your Saviour is longing to bless you,
    There's danger and death in delay.

*   *   *

Printed in the United States of America